all along the Atlantic

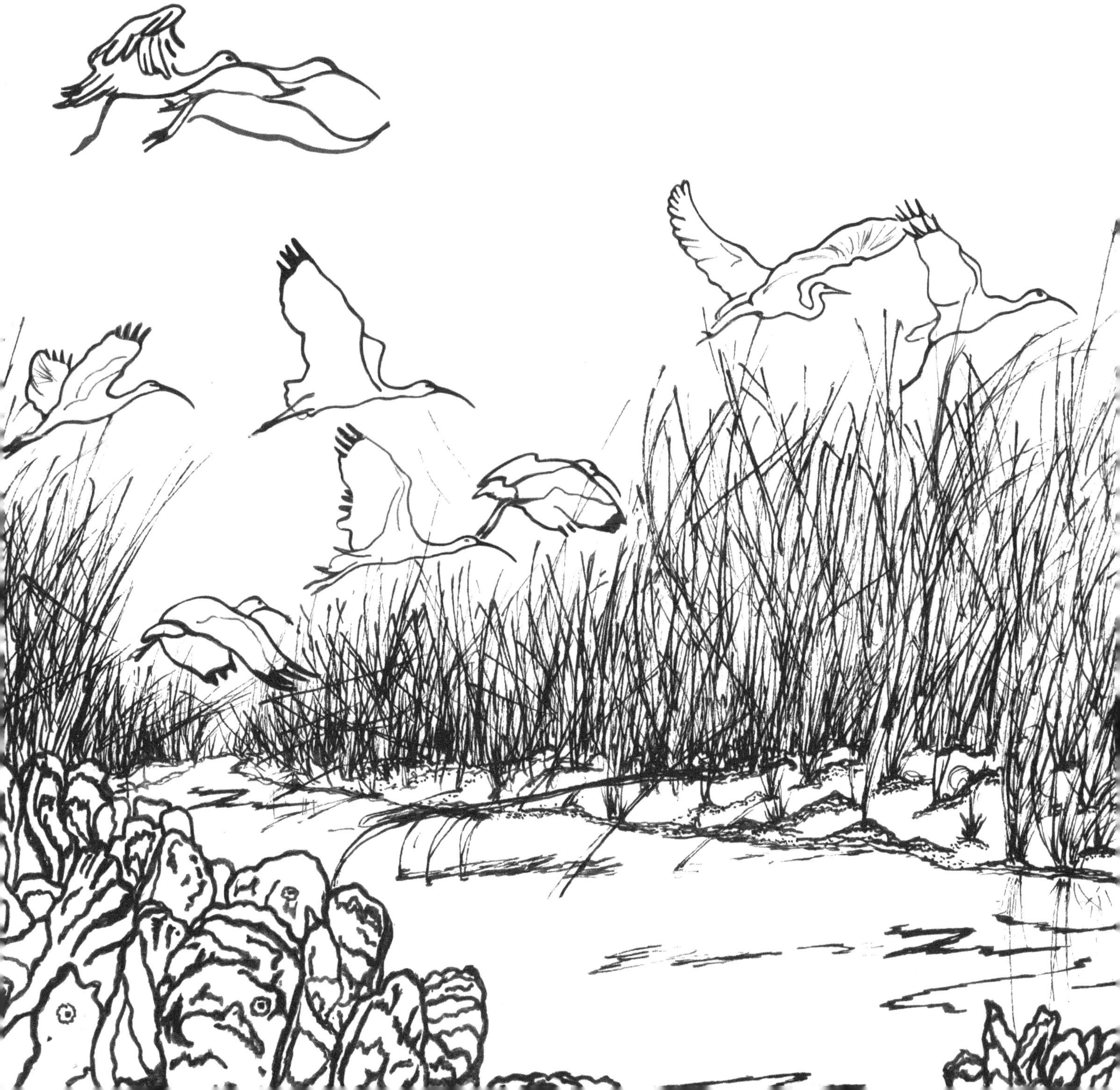

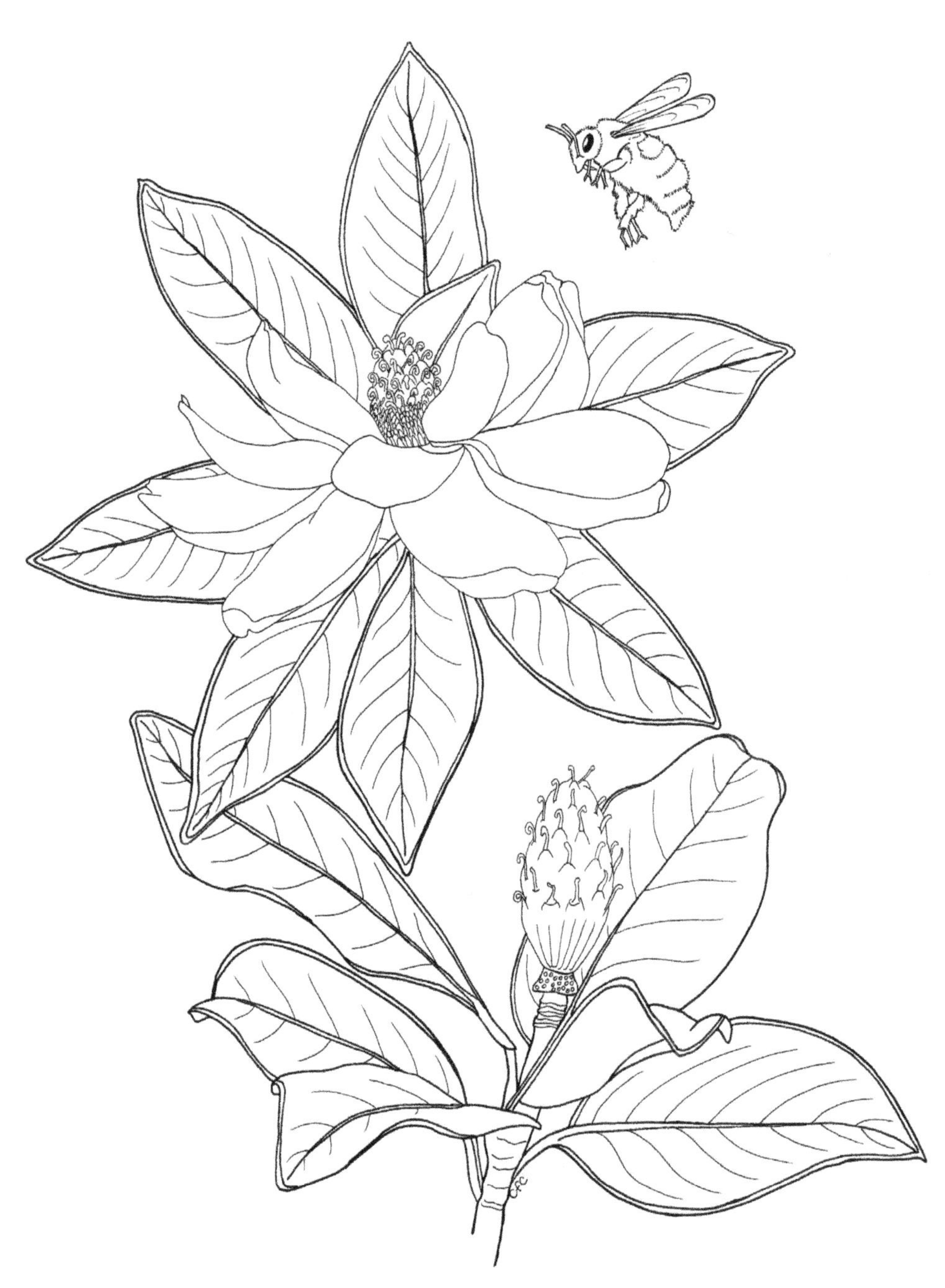

all along the Atlantic

FROM OPEN OCEAN TO CYPRESS SWAMP

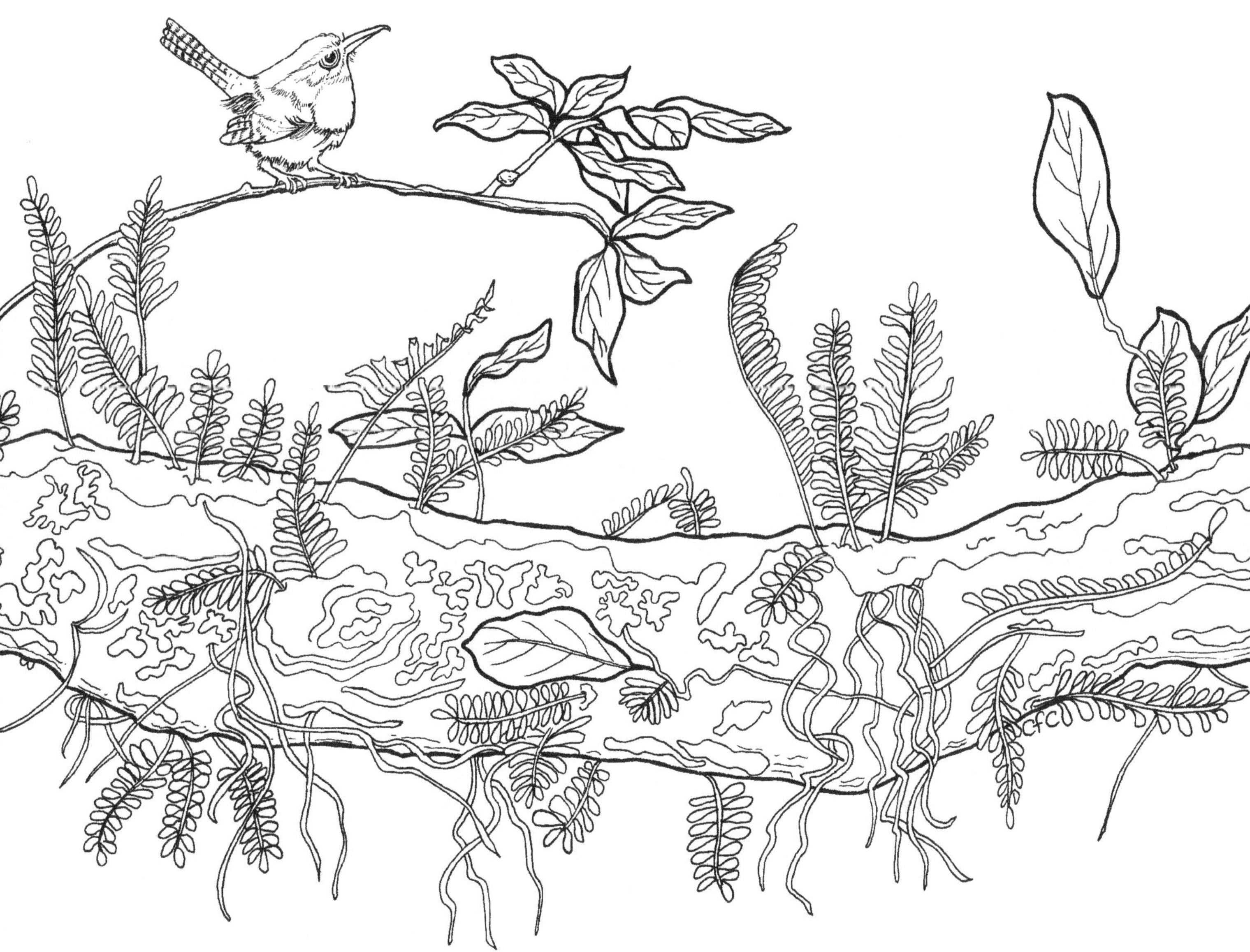

For Peter. May your spirit always be my inspiration...
—Cathy Meyer

For Joseph, Jake, and everyone entranced by the continual miracle of the sea
—Cordelia Norris

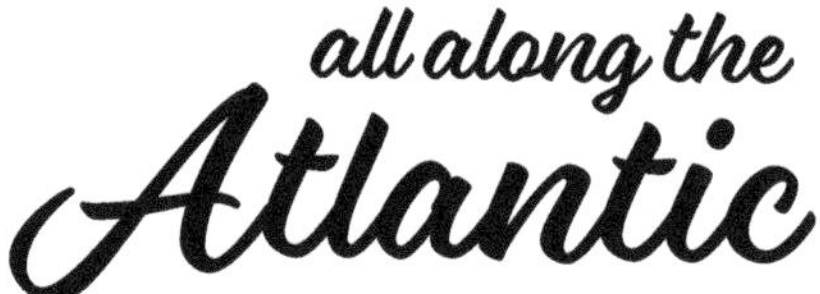

FROM OPEN OCEAN TO CYPRESS SWAMP

Luna Creative in partnership with Old Sins
Wilmington, North Carolina 28409
lunacreates.com

TABLE OF CONTENTS

Coastal waters

Sandy beach

Estuary

Estuary, continued

Wetlands

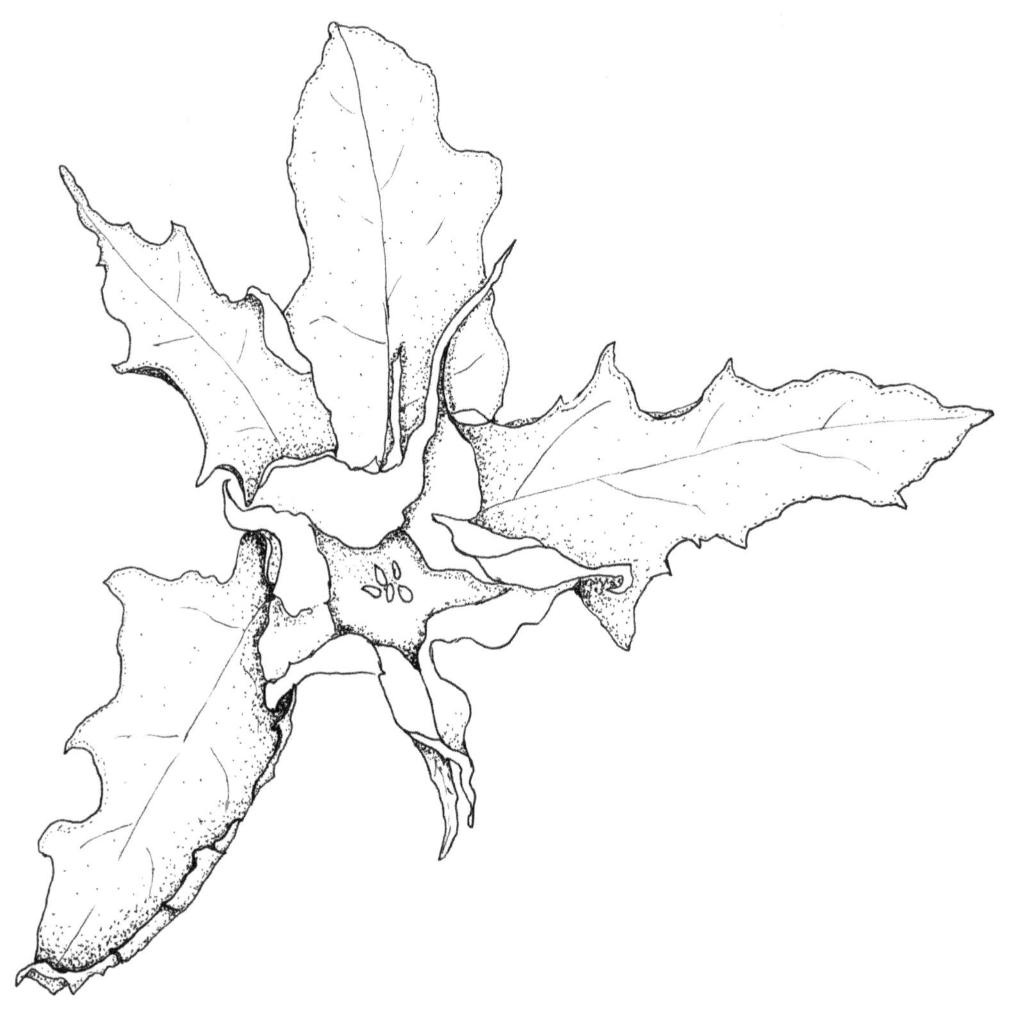

OTHER WORKS BY THE SAME AUTHORS

Cordelia Norris

Hatchlings: A Coloring Book Anthology

Cathy Meyer

Avian-Cetacean Press lead editor on:
Nature Guide to the Carolina Coast, by Peter Meyer
Blue Crabs: Catch 'em, Cook 'em, Eat 'em, by Peter Meyer

Coastwalk North Carolina, by Cathy and Peter Meyer
a 4-part iBook adventure walking the coastal beaches of North Carolina

To me the sea is a continual miracle,
The fishes that swim—the rocks—the motion of the waves—the ships with men in them,
What stranger miracles are there?

—**WALT WHITMAN,** *Miracles*

Our journey begins far offshore in the Atlantic Ocean, moving to the coastal fringes where the sea meets rocky shorelines and sandy beaches. Following the flow of the tide, salty ocean waters collide and mix with freshwater rivers and streams. We move in to brackish estuaries before coming to rest along the edges of the freshwater swamp. The water, land, and air along the Atlantic host an amazing diversity of living organisms, from the tiniest microscopic plankton to the largest animals to ever live on Earth.

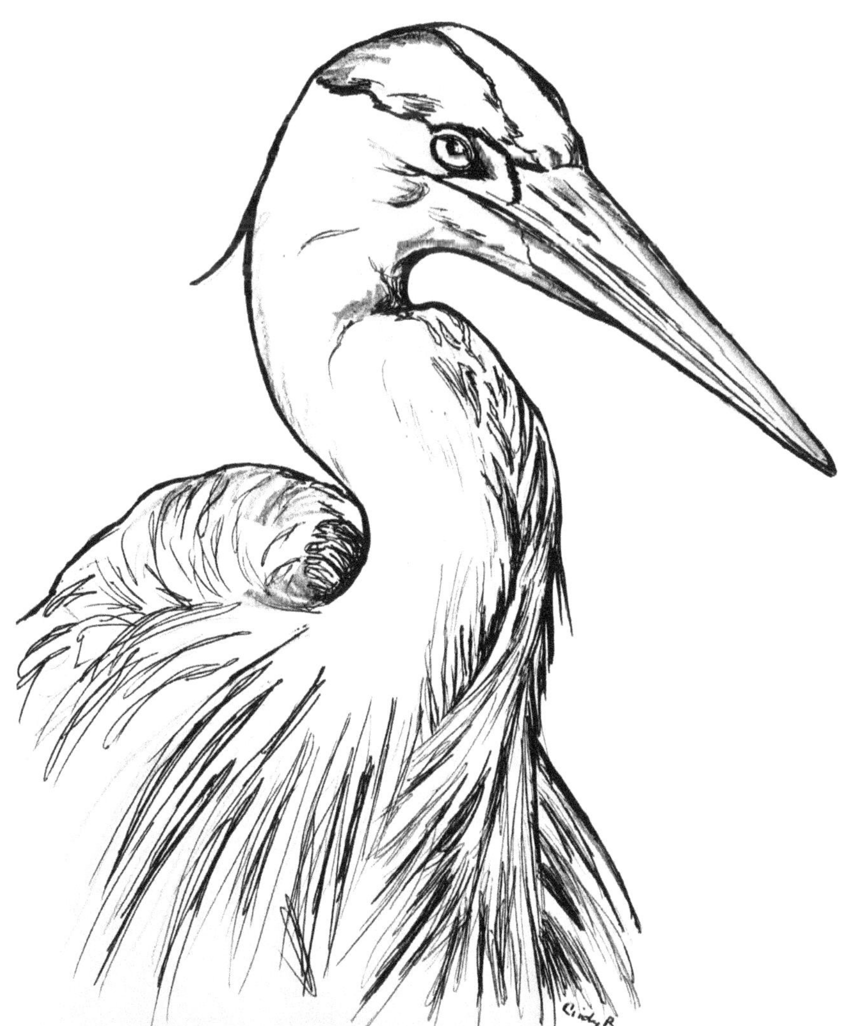

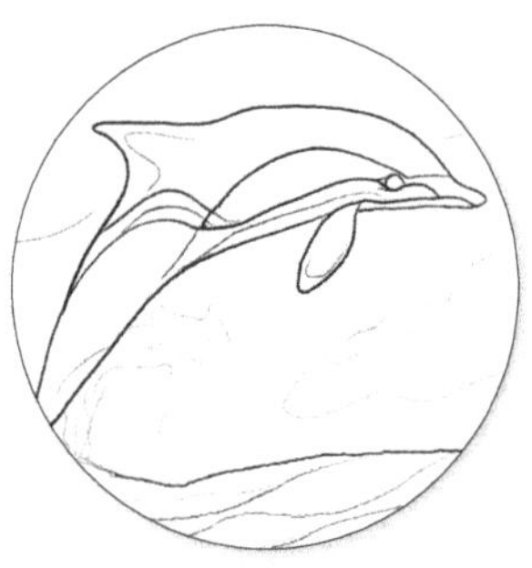

Open ocean

Tina Schofield, illustrator

Far offshore, the continental shelf plunges into the deep sea. Marine life courses through the ocean and along the seafloor below. Thousands of short-beaked dolphins gather together. Marked by dark grey and white hour-glass patterns on their sides, these highly social animals work together to corral schools of herring into a tight mass. Then, coming from underneath, the dolphins take turns swimming into the ball of fish for easy feeding.

During the feeding frenzy, kite-shaped manta rays glide through the depths enjoying their own feast. Scooped-shaped appendages on their heads funnel water full of tiny zooplankton, krill, and small fish into their gaping mouth.

Over one million different species live in Earth's oceans.

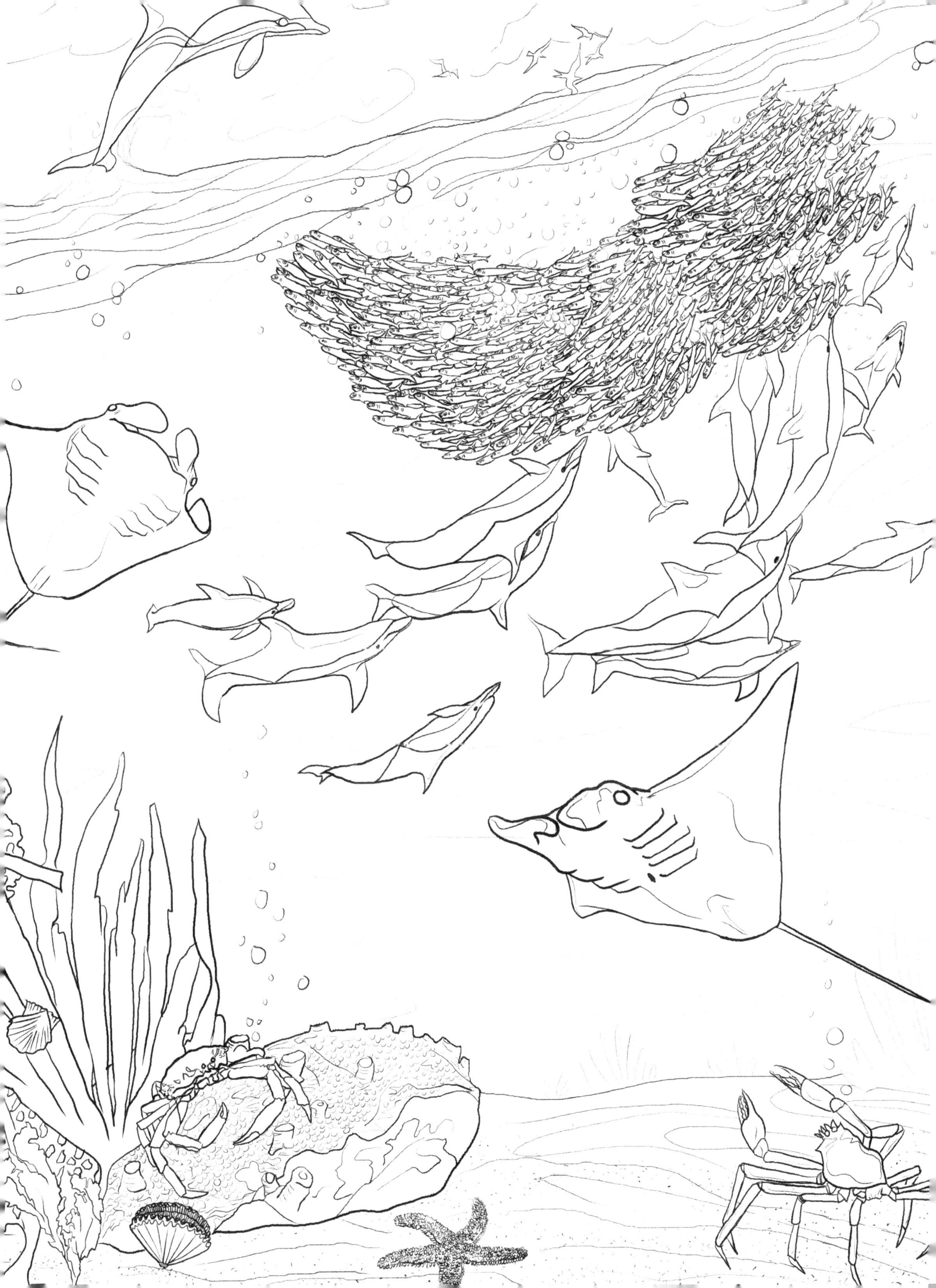

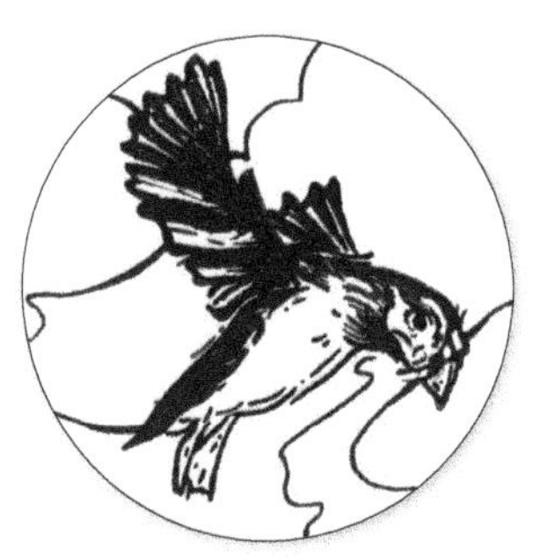

Leviathans of the sea

Cass Graybeal Brown, illustrator

The humpback whale is easily recognized by long pectoral fins and a bumpy head. With pectoral fins extended outward like graceful wings, humpbacks launch themselves out of the water in an arching breach, then turn and fall on their back into the water. Though slow-swimming, these whales migrate over 16,000 miles every year. Cooperating together, humpbacks use a bubble-blowing technique to encircle small fish, tiny krill, and plankton, forcing them together. With a wide-open mouth, the whales come up from beneath the swirl and engulf the trapped prey. Water is pushed out through baleen, leaving only food to be swallowed. Humpbacks, along with all whales and dolphins, are especially sensitive to loud noise. Deep-water seismic blasts are tremendously harmful to these animals.

Atlantic puffins enjoy the same cold ocean areas with humpback whales. These stout, medium-sized birds have colorful bills. They spend most of the year in the open ocean, far offshore, among the coral canyons and seamounts. Most of the time, they are bobbing on the ocean surface or foraging for food while diving underwater. Atlantic puffins are only found on isolated rocky islands off the northeastern coast during their 4-month summer nesting season.

The male humpback whales are known for their hauntingly beautiful songs that may last 20 minutes or go on for hours.

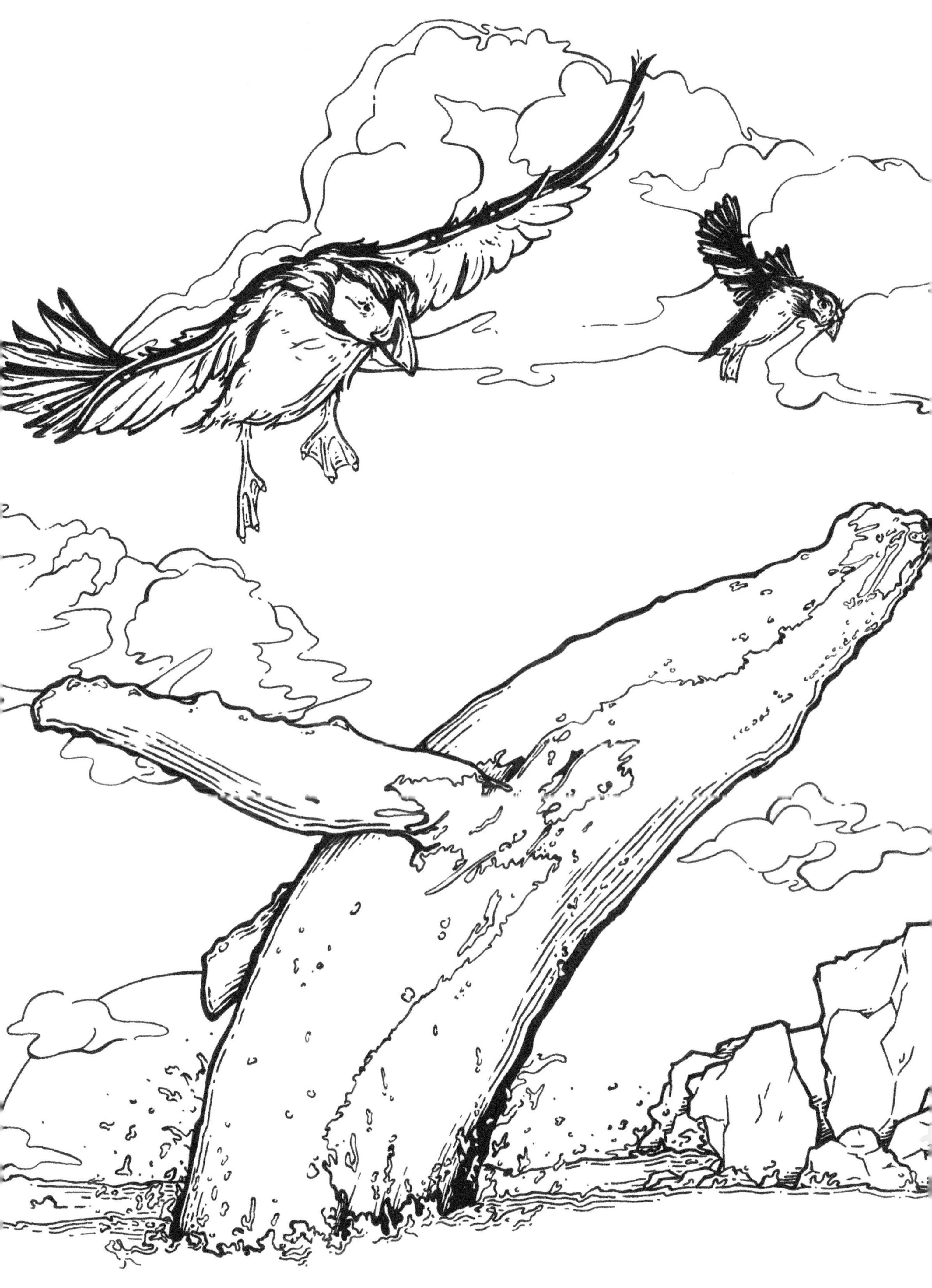

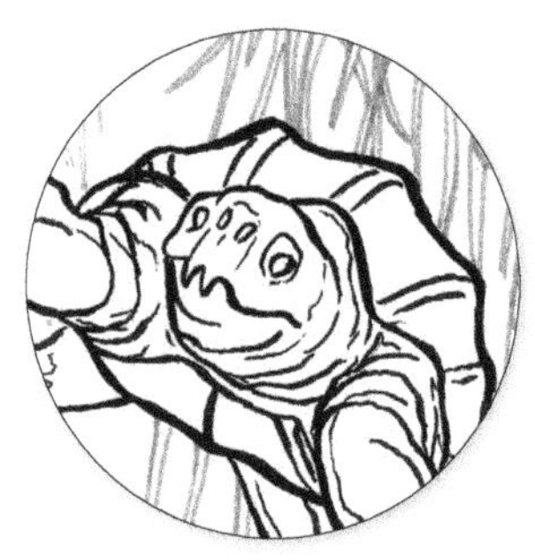

Marathon swimmers

Tiffany Miller Russell, illustrator

Leatherback sea turtles are the largest living turtles on Earth. The flippers are exceedingly long in proportion to the body. The shell is exceptionally hydrodynamic in design. Instead of bony scutes, like other turtles, the shell is covered with a smooth, leathery layer of skin. These features help the turtle achieve extreme diving depths of 4,200 feet. Leatherbacks are long-distance swimmers. They constantly swim at a slow, steady pace through the ocean. Their migration routes from feeding grounds to nesting areas may cover over 3,000 miles. All sea turtles have lungs and must surface frequently to breathe air, but leatherbacks can stay underwater for 85 minutes. They feed along the surface and during deep dives. Lion's mane jellies and Portuguese man-of-war are among their favorite foods. Downward-pointing spines, called papillae, line the throat of leatherbacks and keep the gelatinous food from coming back out of the mouth. Sea turtles have thick skin around their beak-like mouth that protects them from the sting of jellies and man-of-wars.

A dead leatherback sea turtle was found with 11 pounds of plastic debris in its stomach.

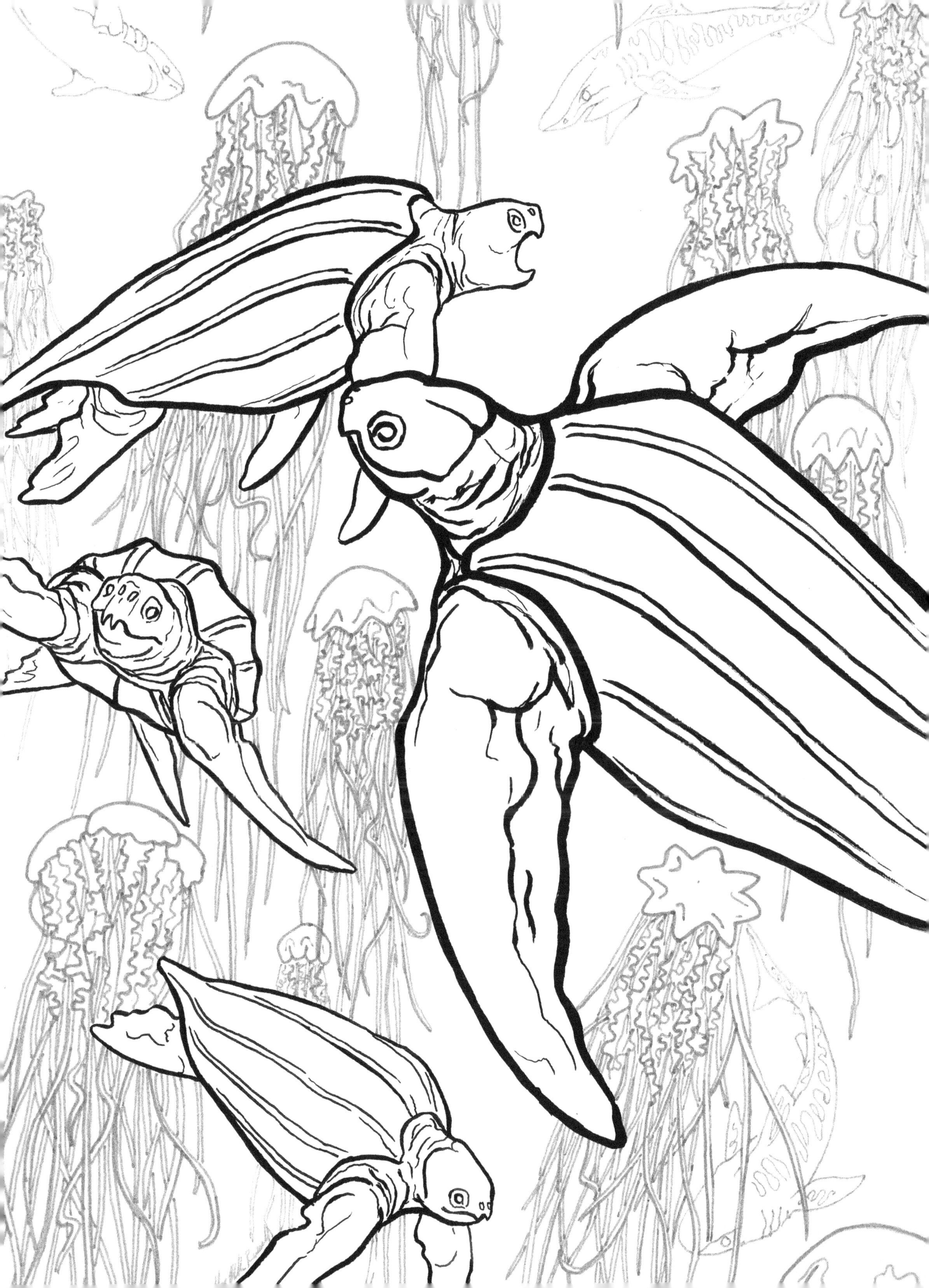

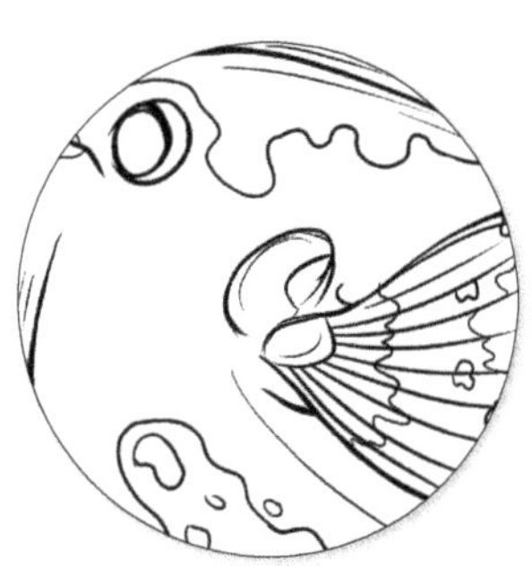

Sunning on the sea

Madi Henline, illustrator

Ranking as the heaviest of all bony fish, ocean sunfish (or molas) can weigh up to 5,000 pounds. These heavyweights are about the size of a flattened refrigerator swimming in the ocean. However, molas don't start out that big. Tiny as a pinhead when hatched, molas grow to 60 million times larger than that by the time they are adults. They must eat a lot of food to obtain this enormous size. Diving down 650 feet, molas snack on jellies, Portuguese man-of-war, small fish, squid, sponges, and a tremendous amount of zooplankton along the way. In order to warm up after deep dives, these silvery fish often sunbathe on the ocean surface. A fish this size can't keep parasites from latching on for free rides. Molas seek out floating kelp mats where resident cleaner fish will help remove the pests. Gulls often help out with the pest removal process while the ocean sunfish are basking on the ocean surface. Molas are docile creatures, and generally just go with the flow.

One female ocean sunfish can spawn 300 million eggs at a time.

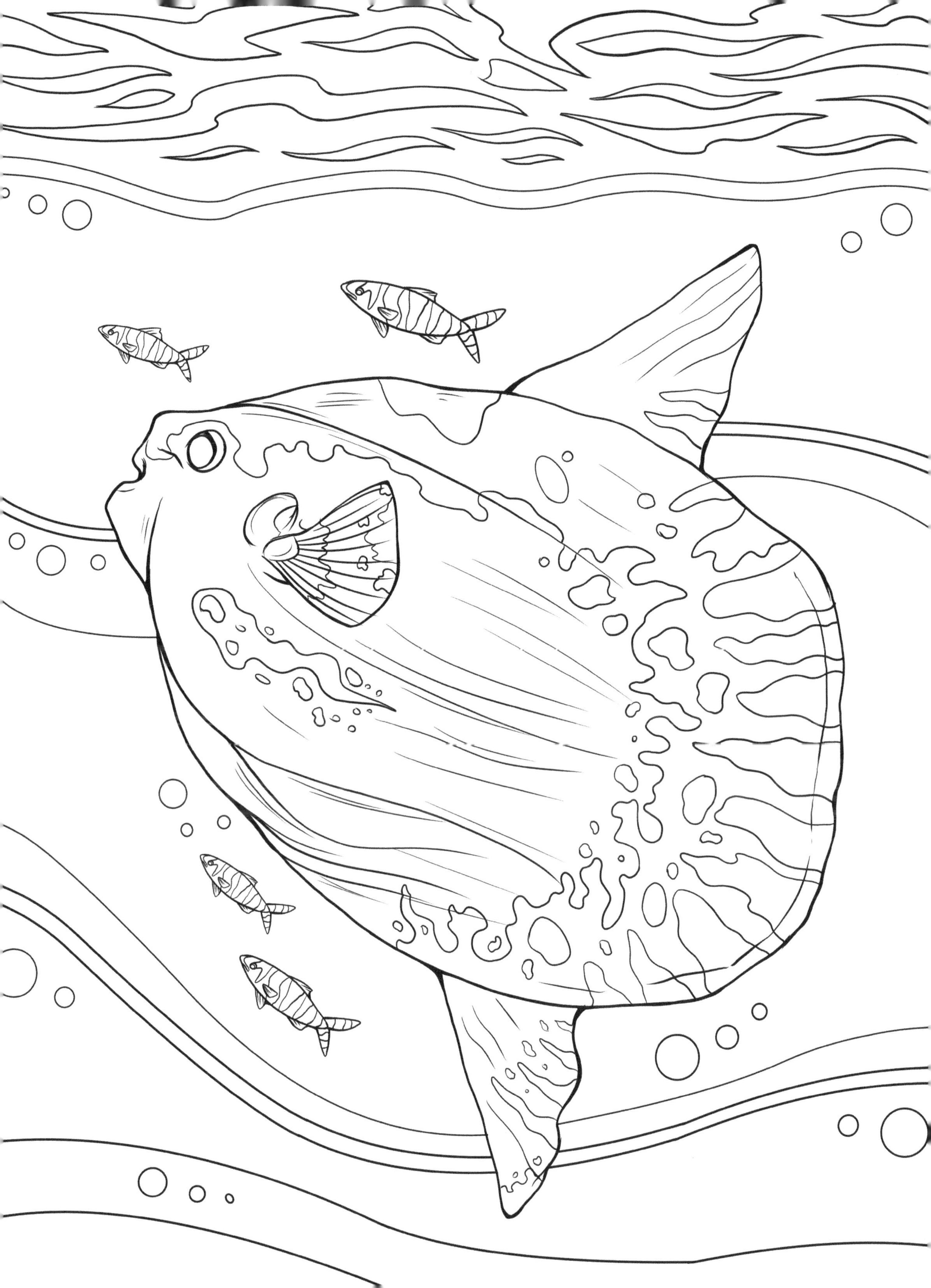

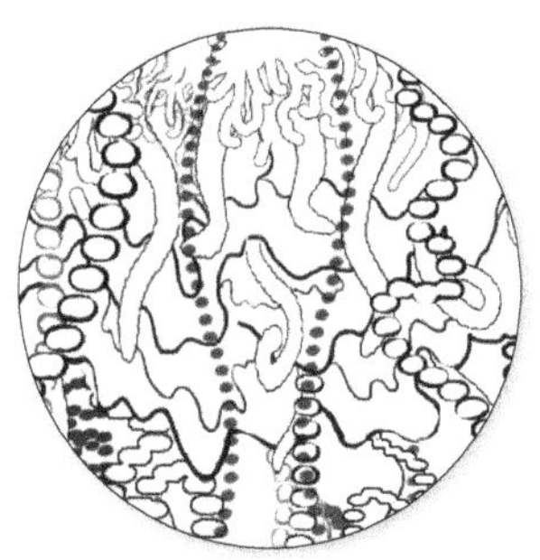

Armed with venom

Christina Spence Morgan, illustrator

Cnidarians have tentacles armed with nematocysts, stinging cells filled with paralyzing venom ready to fire with the slightest touch. Depending on the size or species of cnidarian, the target can be any fish or plankton that gets too close to the trailing tentacles. An unsuspecting victim is stunned by venom. The cnidarian coils its tentacles around the motionless body, injecting more venom into the catch. The prey is disintegrating by the time the tentacles deliver the meal to the cnidarian's mouth.

Cnidaria is the scientific phylum classification for jellyfish, sea anemones, corals, and hydrozoans. There are two body forms of cnidarians: medusae and polyps. Medusae have a mouth located on the underside of an umbrella-shaped dome with tentacles attached around the rim of the dome. Jellyfish, such as lion's mane and sea nettles, are well-known medusae. Polyps have a tubular body that is anchored in place with their mouth and tentacles located on the top. Some polyps live by themselves, like sea anemones. Others prefer a communal living arrangement, like corals. Hydrozoans have both medusa and polyp stages. They may be a solitary creature or a specialized colony floating together as a single entity, like Portuguese man-of-war and by-the-wind sailors.

Blue glaucous is a brightly colored nudibranch, also called a blue dragon. The blue dragon feeds on Portuguese man-of-wars, storing the stinging nematocysts in its own body. When touched, the blue dragon releases a highly concentrated dose of stinging cells to protect itself.

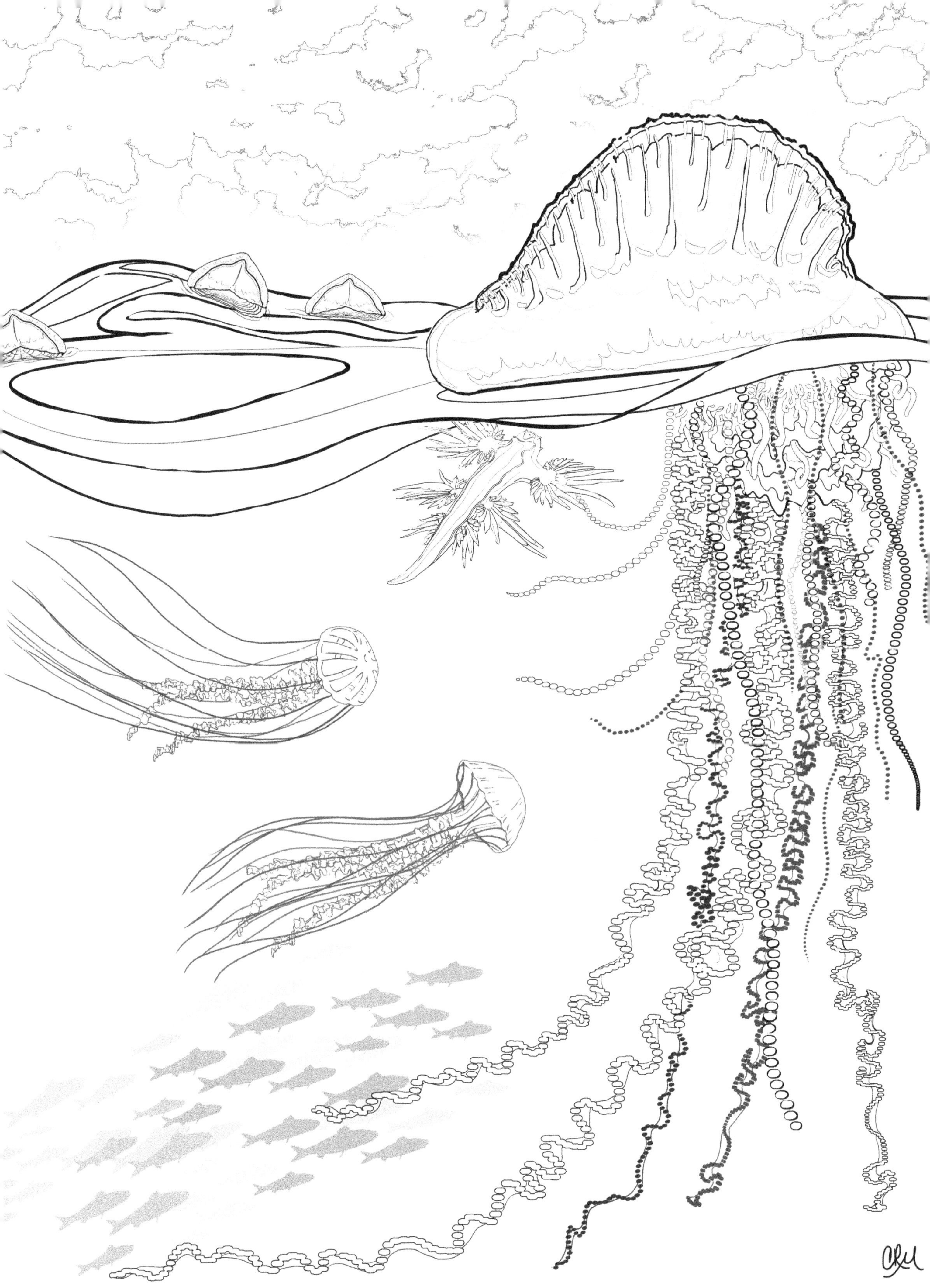

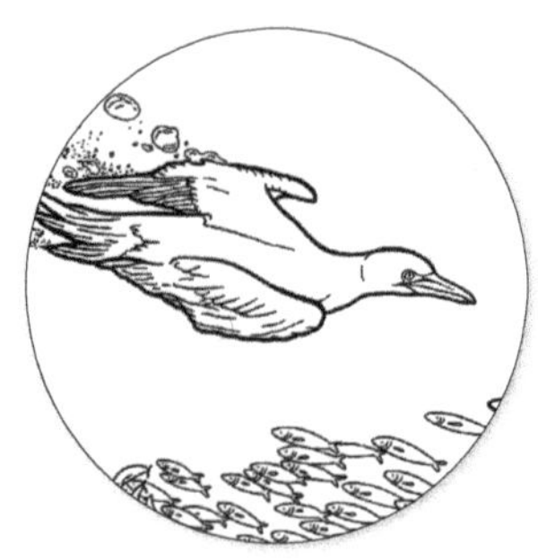

Feeding frenzy

Elizabeth Bonert, illustrator

Cooperative hunting is a technique often used by bluefin tuna and Atlantic white-sided dolphins. They chase a large number of small fish, like herring and mackerel, into a small area. The corralled fish swim in a tight circle, forming what looks like a large ball. With a tight swirling bait ball, the predators have an easy time catching more fish to eat. Tuna will attack from the sides, dolphins from below. It's not only aquatic predators that benefit from this hunting technique, but birds like northern gannets take advantage of the tightly compacted quantity of fish near the surface for easy picking.

Things can get pretty crazy during a feeding frenzy. Panic sets into the swirling mass of fish and the surface of the water breaks into an agitation of boiling waves. Mayhem ensues as the fish ball is attacked from above and below. By the time the frenzy settles, casualties will be many and attackers may suffer injuries as well.

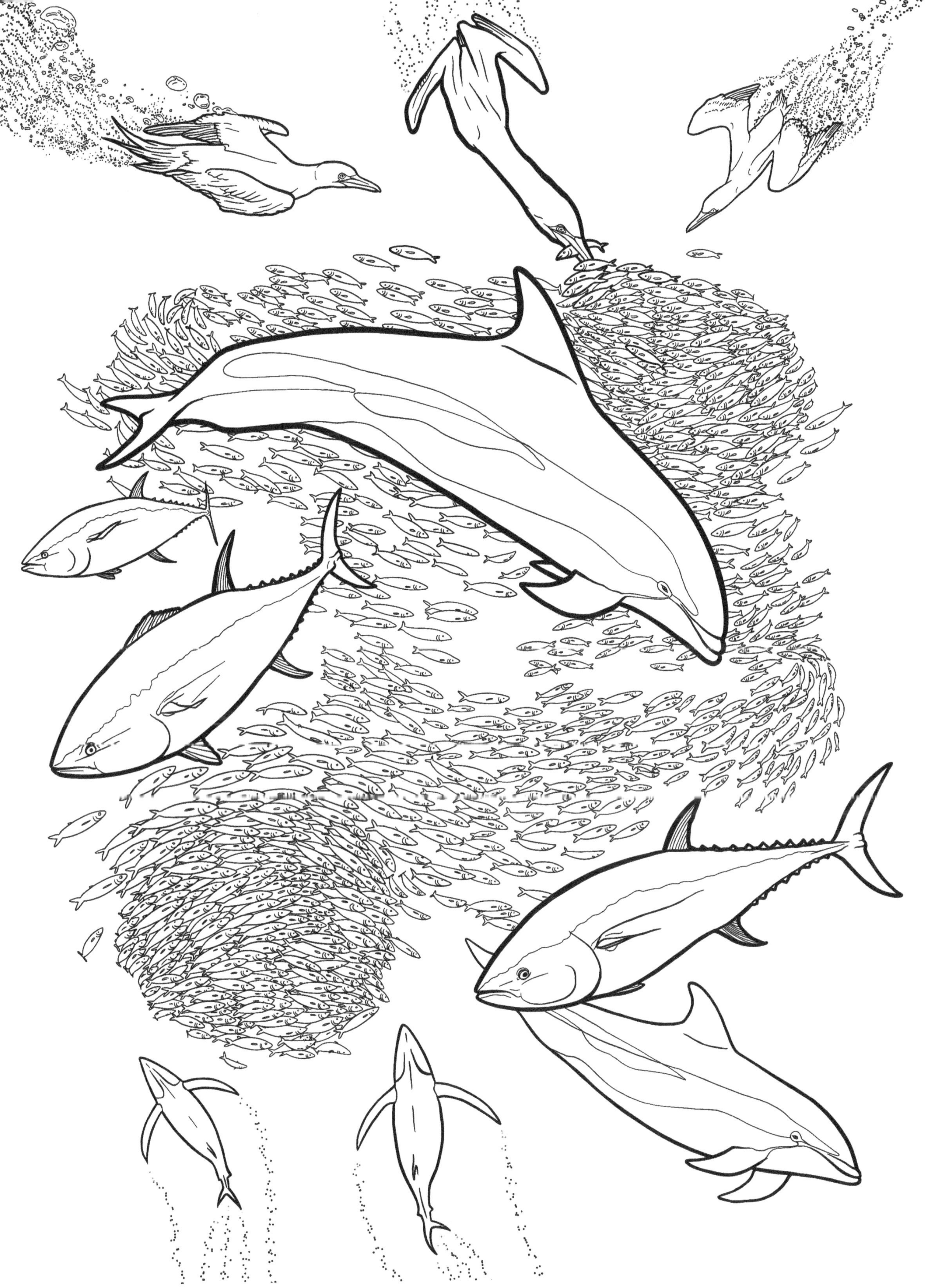

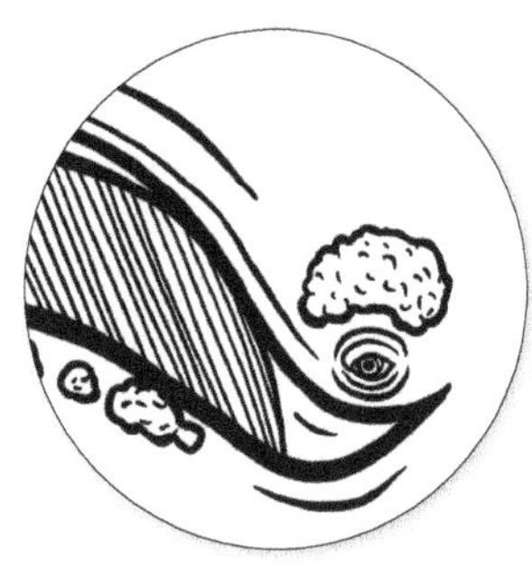

On the verge of extinction

Elizabeth Bonert, illustrator

With possibly as few as 400 remaining in the North Atlantic Ocean, the North Atlantic right whale is the most endangered whale species in the world. Right whales are dark gray, bulky-looking baleen whales, about the size of a tractor-trailer. Patchy areas of skin on their heads, called callosities, form unique patterns covered with white whale lice. Scientists are able to identify individual whales by these markings. Right whales migrate along the eastern seaboard, with a tendency to stay close to the coast. Traveling alone or in small groups on migration routes, right whales may cover more than 1,000 miles from the cold waters of the Canadian and New England coasts before reaching warm waters off the southern coasts for the winter. They skim the surface of the ocean for small invertebrates such as copepods, krill, and larval barnacles.

Copepods, krill, and larval barnacles are small invertebrates ranging in size from barely one millimeter up to 20 centimeters. Copepods are found just about anywhere there is water, salty or fresh. Krill depend on sea ice and cold ocean water temperatures to survive. Barnacles begin life as free-swimming zooplankton, then undergo metamorphosis before anchoring in place. These invertebrates, along with many thousand others, are a vital link in the global food chain, feasting on algae, phytoplankton, and bacteria before being consumed by hundreds of different species in the sea.

The largest animals in the sea, including blue whales, humpback whales, whale sharks, and manta rays, feed on microscopic plankton and krill.

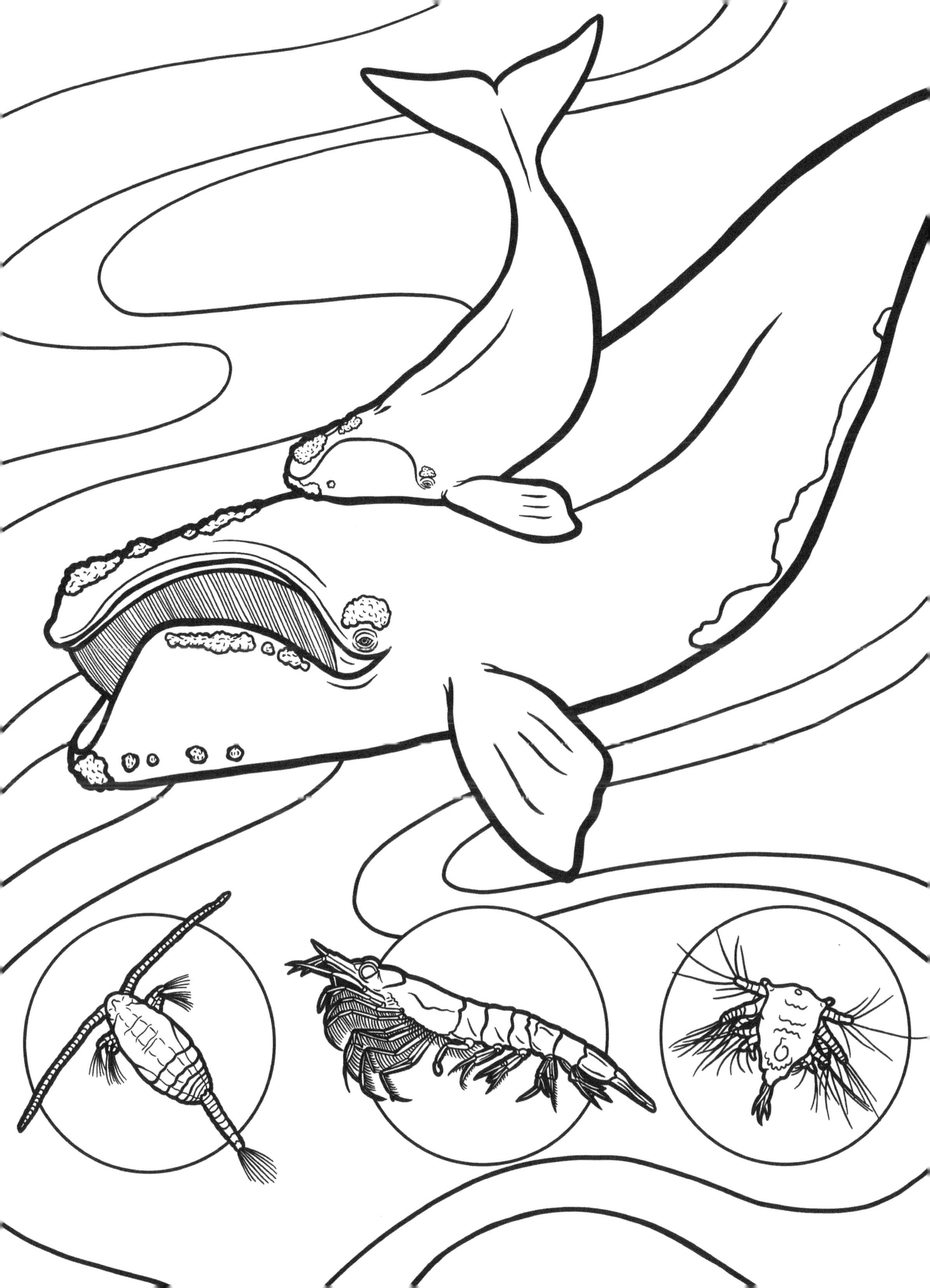

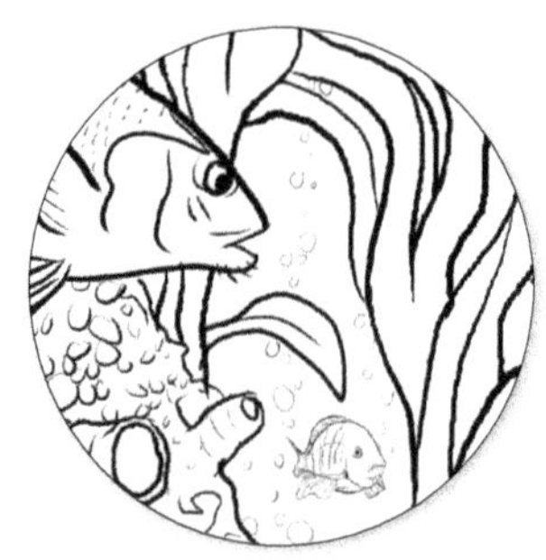

Underwater forests

Tina Schofield, illustrator

Kelp forests are usually associated with the Pacific coast, but the northern Atlantic has its own version of this underwater ecosystem. Several different species of large brown algae, such as sugar kelp and horsetail kelp, anchor to the seafloor and reach up toward the surface through the cold, nutrient-rich water. Kelp forests are one of the most productive ecosystems in the ocean, providing key habitats and food for a diverse array of species. Kelp forests also provide important nursery areas for different fish species and safe hiding places from large predators like sandbar sharks.

For more than five centuries, the Atlantic cod was an abundantly available fish in the sea that drove the economy in coastal Canada and New England. Advanced fishing-finding technology introduced in the 1950s resulted in extensive overfishing of Atlantic cod. The cod fishery collapsed in the 1990s. Enormous volumes of other fish species that were incidental by-catch had also been removed along with the cod from the ocean's ecosystems. Without cod and other important fish in the ocean, there are no major predators left to keep the sea urchin population in check. The imbalance is creating a strain on the delicate kelp forest ecosystem, contributing to a rapid decline in the ecosystem's health.

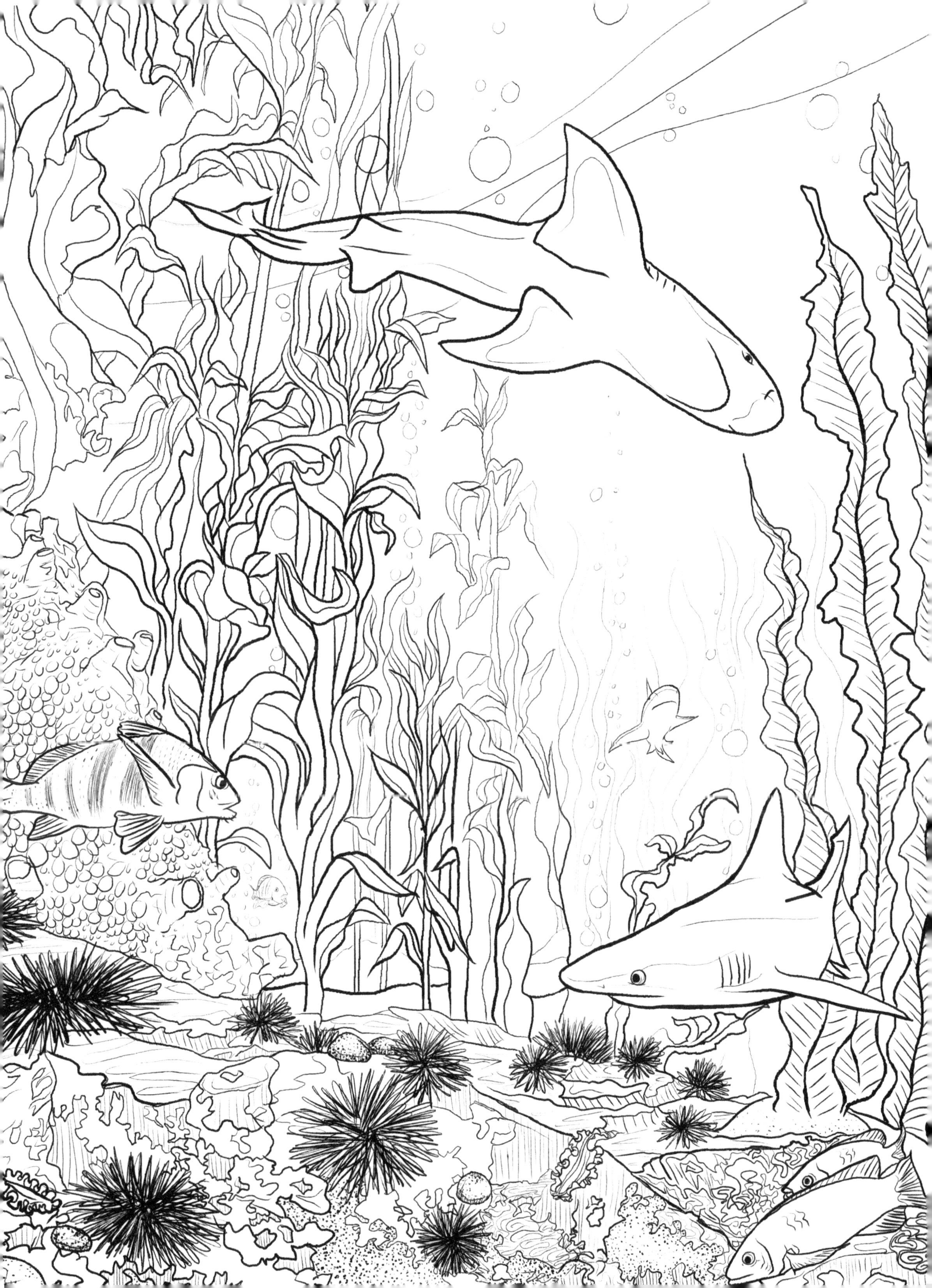

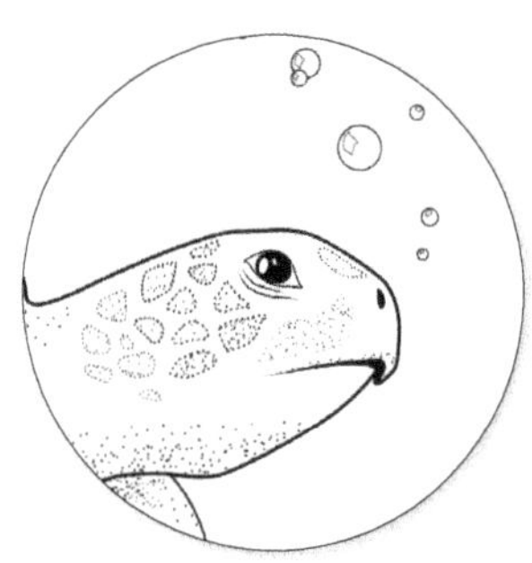

Sea gardener

Kara Perilli, illustrator

Green sea turtles are found throughout the world's oceans. They are named for their greenish-colored cartilage and body fat, not the color of their carapace. Adult green sea turtles have a heart-shaped carapace that measures about five feet in length. Newly hatched green sea turtles begin life about palm size, eating worms, shrimp, crabs, aquatic insects, jellyfish, sponges, seagrasses, and algae. By the time they reach eight to ten inches in length, their diet becomes herbivorous, eating only seagrasses and algae. Their sharp beak has developed serrated edges to aid with tearing plants while foraging. Green sea turtles live in areas with seagrass beds and rarely venture into the open ocean. Green sea turtles are listed as an endangered species—their population has been significantly reduced due to human-caused factors, such as being entangled in fishing nets, ingesting plastic debris, nesting ground destruction, boat propeller collisions, and both egg and turtle poaching for human consumption.

Green sea turtles carefully maintain seagrass beds. Like gardeners, they keep the seagrass trimmed and the algae in check. As a result, seagrass beds stay healthy and productive as nursery areas for important commercial seafood species.

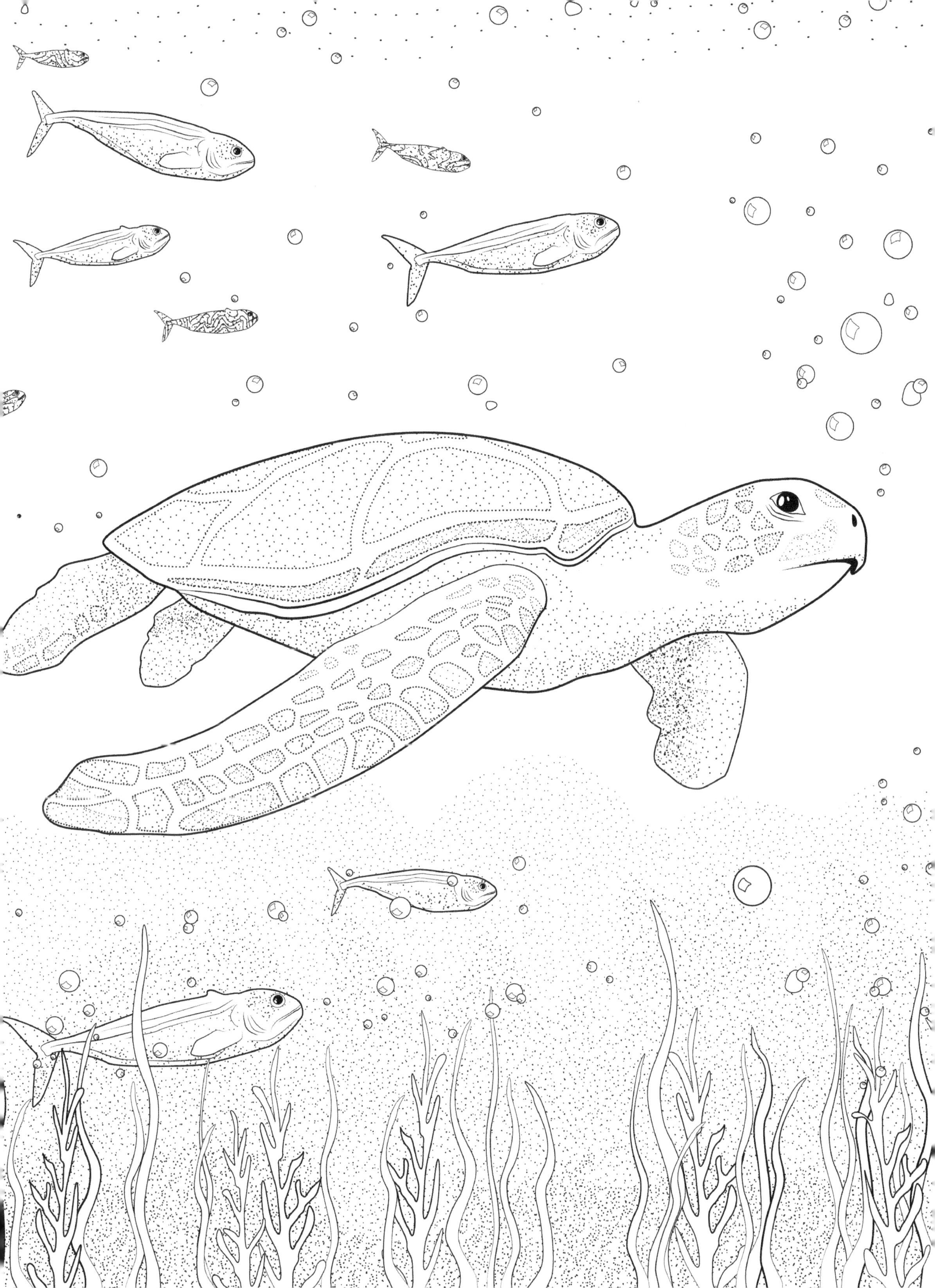

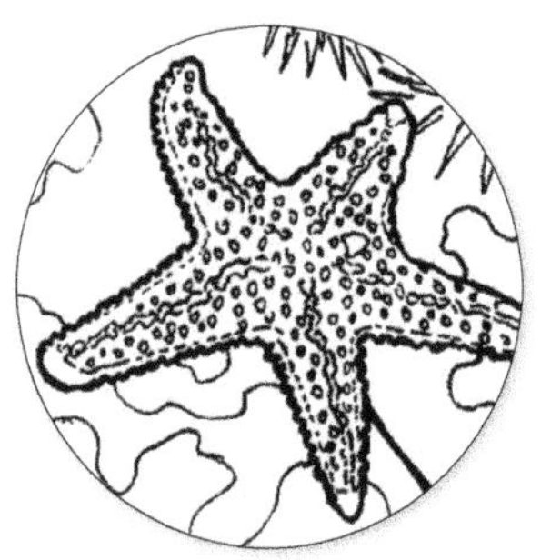

Stars of the sea

Alisa Singh, illustrator

Echinoderms are the stars of the sea. They are animals that include not only sea stars and sea urchins, but brittles stars, sand dollars, and sea cucumbers as well. They all have a body divided into five symmetrical parts that resembles a star, a water vascular system that propels a series of tube feet, and a shell made of calcium carbonate covered by a spiny layer of skin.

Over 2,000 species of sea stars live in the world's oceans and estuaries. Sea stars are capable of regenerating a lost arm or even a whole new body from a severed arm. Some species have more than five arms, but their arm count is usually a multiple of five. Sea stars are found along rocky shorelines or sandy bottoms in the intertidal area, where they feed on clams, oysters, snails, and dead fish. Sea stars will venture into estuaries, staying near ocean inlets along rock jetties and oyster reefs.

Green sea urchins resemble pin cushions, with tube feet located in between protruding spines. They are found close to shore, in rocky crevices and reefs throughout the intertidal area, feeding on algae and decomposing organic matter.

A sea star can travel about one mile in a week.

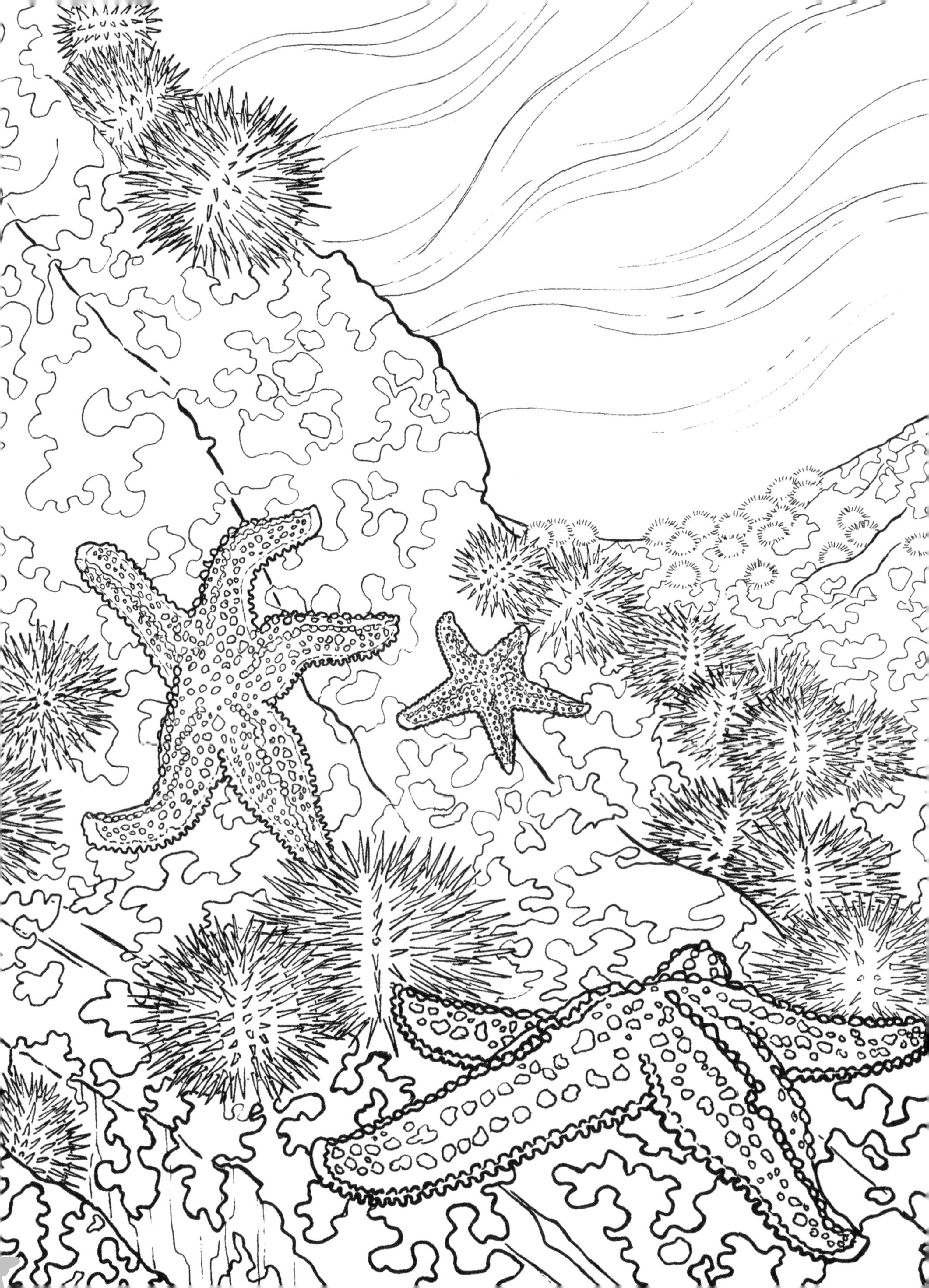

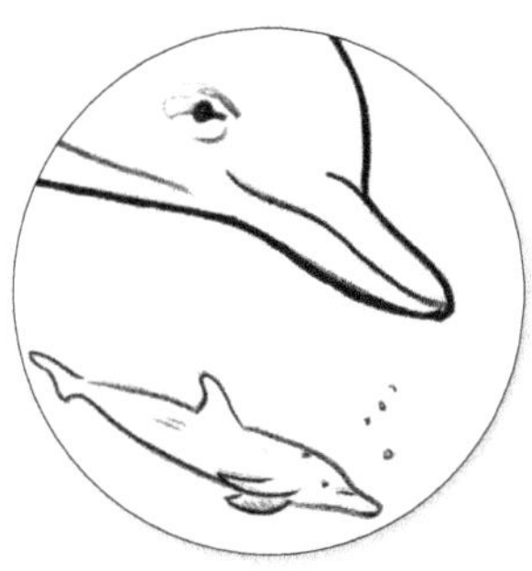

Charismatic cetacean

Amanda Surveski, illustrator

These charismatic cetaceans, also known as the Atlantic bottlenose dolphins, are found throughout the Atlantic Ocean and around the world. Staying primarily close to the coast, they will venture into estuaries, as well as harbors, bays, and gulfs, just about anywhere there is brackish water deep enough with food for them to eat. Often hunting as a group, they will corral fish into a tight circle for easier pickings. Dolphins will snag fish in their teeth, and then swallow the fish, head first. Squid, crabs, and shrimp are also among their food supply. Bottlenose dolphins can be found alone or in small groups as they travel farther offshore during migrations. Highly intelligent and very social among themselves, this species of dolphin is quite curious and will often approach people and boats to investigate. Dolphins spend their entire life in the water, and are able to swim from the moment they are born. They are mammals and must breathe air by surfacing several times every few minutes. Bottlenose dolphins are able to dive deeply and stay submerged for long periods of time, but they generally stay higher in the water column when food is available.

Dolphins are toothed cetaceans, like porpoises, orcas, sperm whales, and pilot whales.

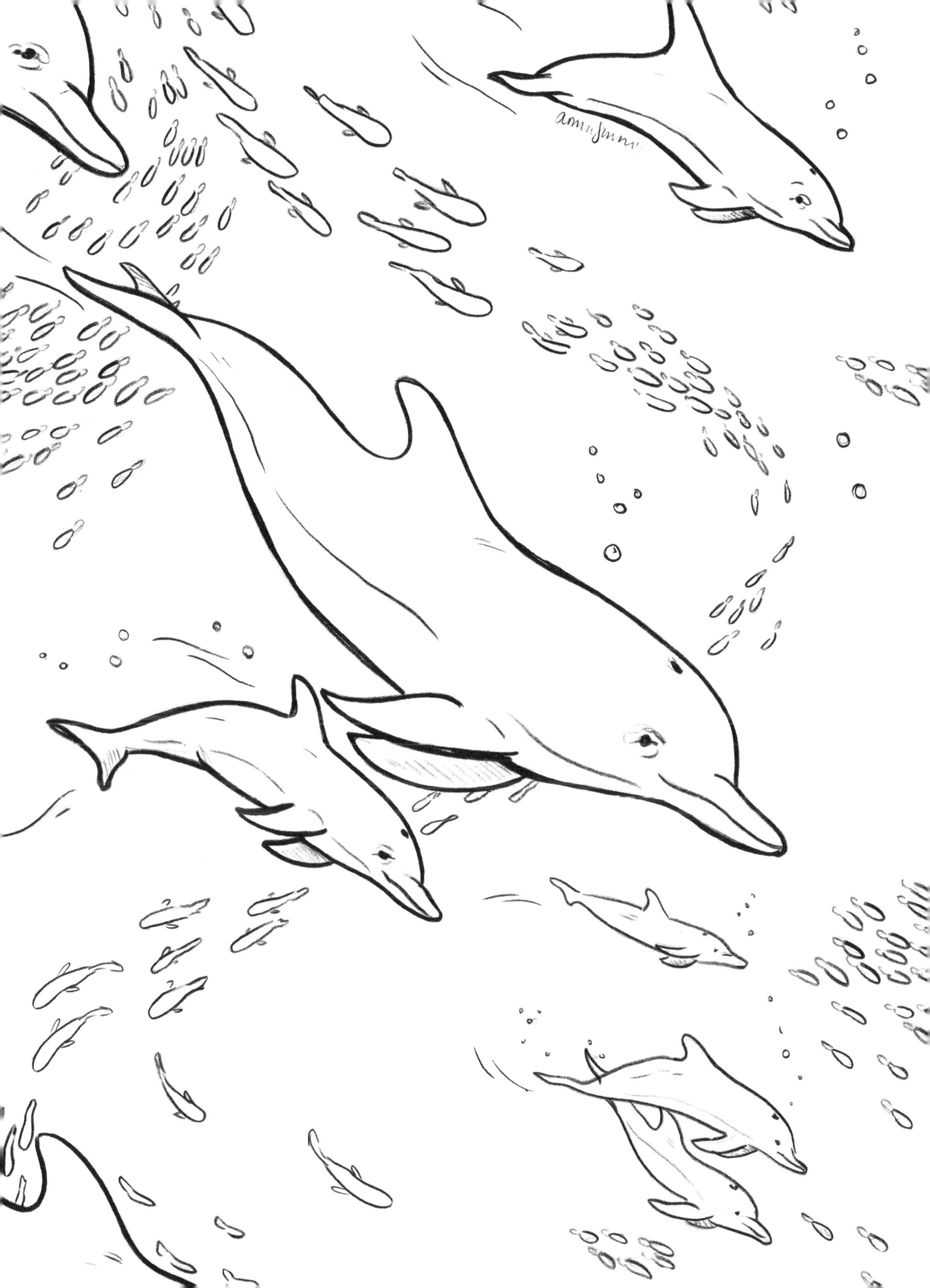

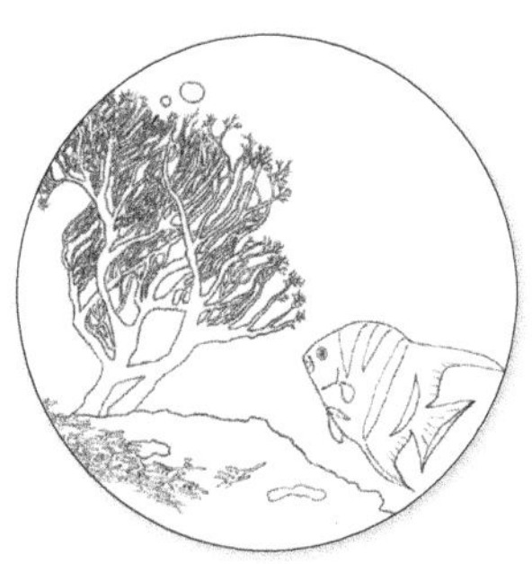

At home in the sea

Bonnie Cadotte, illustrator

Loggerhead sea turtles are found in the open ocean, as well as coastal waters and estuaries. Like all sea turtles, the loggerhead has lungs and must surface every five to fifteen minutes to breathe air. The thick, stumpy head that pops out of the water looks like a floating log. That is why they are called loggerheads. Loggerheads have powerful jaws that enable them to crush and eat hard-shelled animals, such as crabs, whelks and other mollusks, sea urchins, and horseshoe crabs. Jellyfish, squid, fish, and even sargassum and other seaweed are part of their diet. The loggerhead turtle's shell is about three feet in length and is often host to over a hundred different species of animals and plants along for a free ride through the ocean. Because this sea turtle hangs out within fifteen feet of the surface, collisions with boat propellers are often fatal. Loggerheads may be the most abundant sea turtle in the ocean, but they are still protected by the Endangered Species Act.

Marine debris, especially floating plastic bags and balloons, resembles many favorite foods for marine animals. Ingested marine debris can block the gastrointestinal tract, keeping food from being digested properly. Loggerhead turtles with plastics in their stomach cannot release their digestive gases. Those gases build up inside the body and keep them afloat on the surface. This condition is called Floater Syndrome. Unable to dive or adequately swim, the turtles are more susceptible to predator attacks and boat strikes.

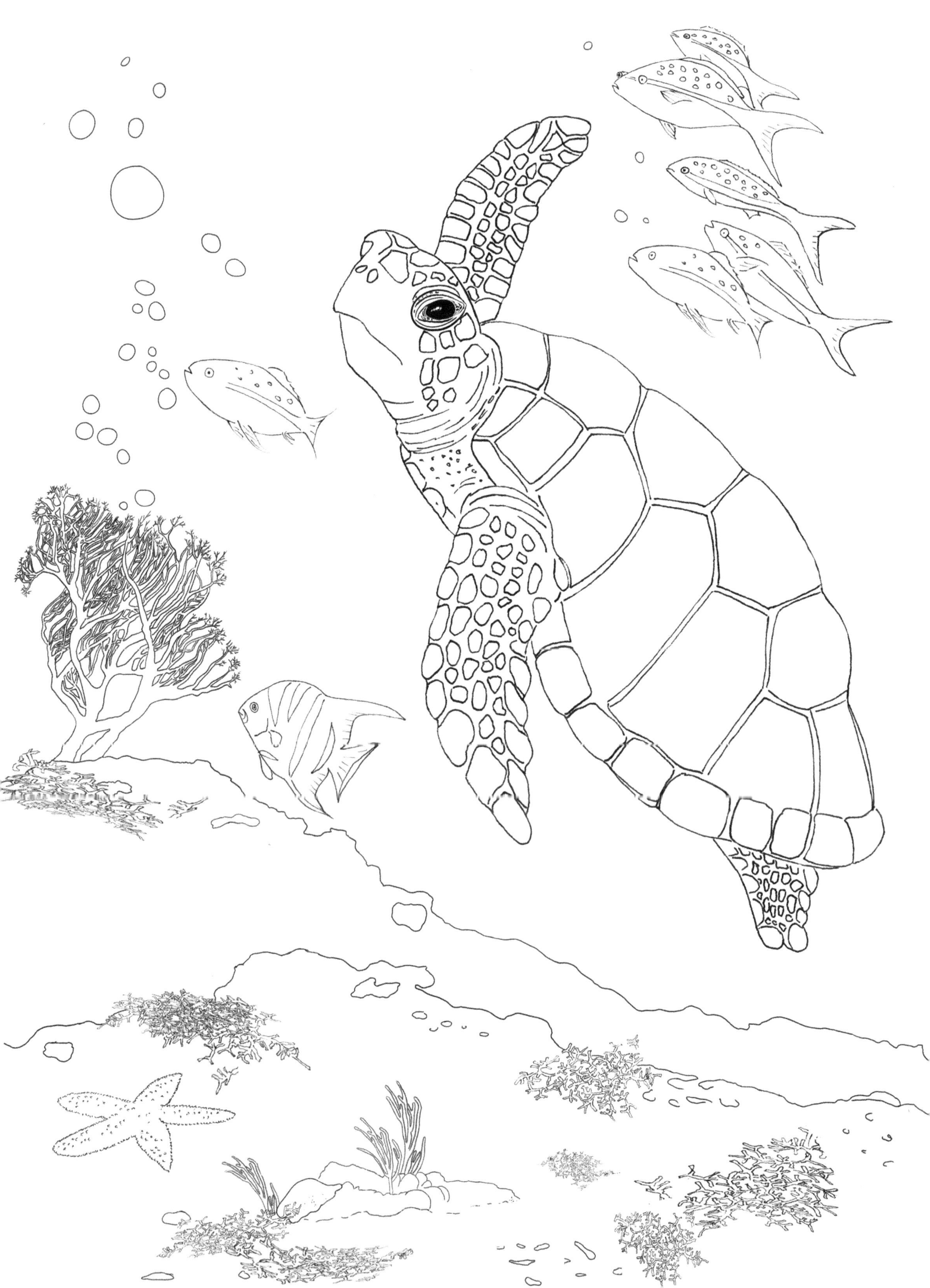

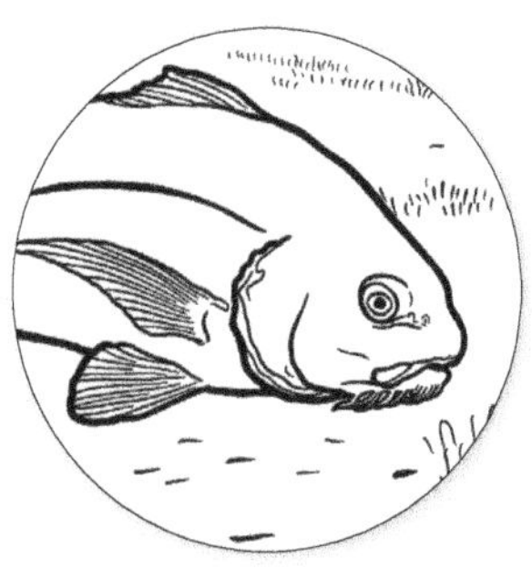

Inshore secrets

Elizabeth Bonert, illustrator

Close to shore, where the ocean is no deeper than 30-35 feet, is generally considered inshore waters. Many species that thrive inshore also frequent the calmer estuary waters. Cownose rays, black drum, and horseshoe crabs are a few creatures that are at home inshore and in the estuary. Cownose rays look like brown kites with a long whip-like tail flying through the ocean and estuaries. Its blunted snout has an indentation resembling a cow's nose. At the base of the tail, a venomous barb sits on top and is used purely for defense. The ray whips the tail up to impale an attacking predator, injecting a toxic venom that causes considerable pain. Cownose rays feed along the seafloor, looking for clams and oysters, gastropods, lobsters, and crabs. They migrate in large groups along the Atlantic coast. Black drum are another species that prefers both the inshore waters and estuaries. They spend their early years in the estuary before moving to inshore waters. Black drum gather around inlets and river mouths to spawn in early spring, so the hatching fry will be swept into the estuary.

Resembling flattened helmets with a long spiked tail, horseshoe crabs have been swimming in Earth's oceans for over 450 million years.

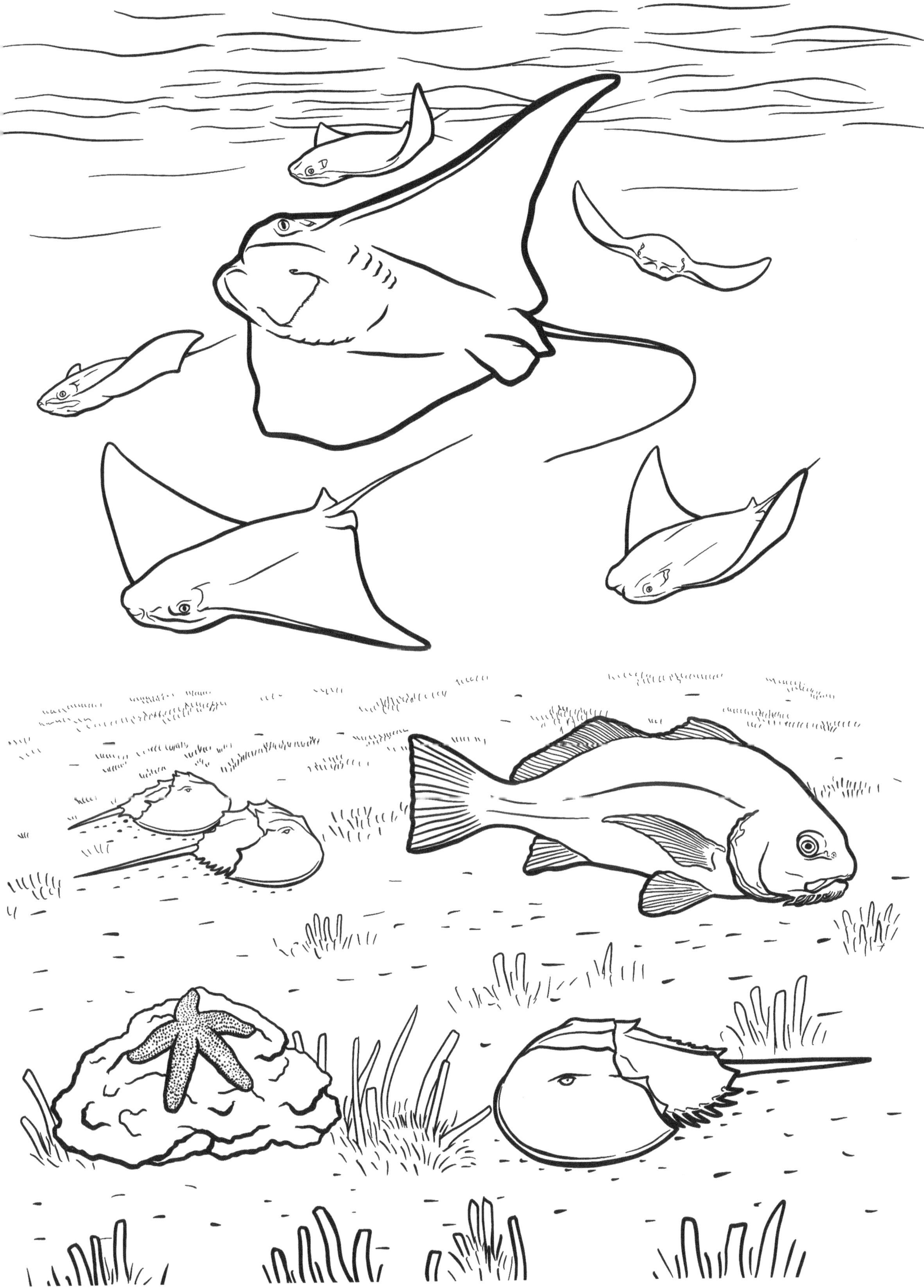

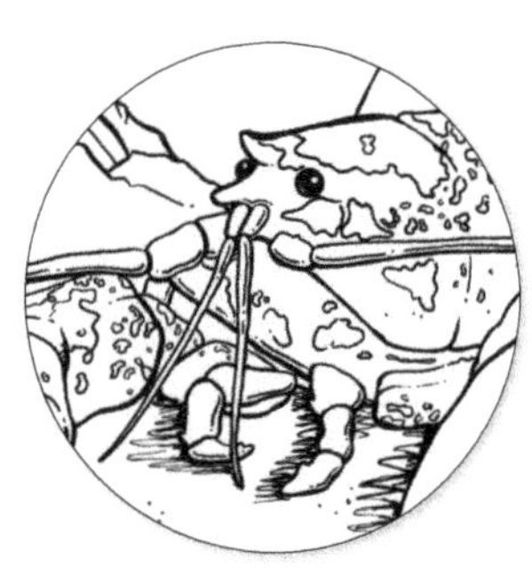

Rocky seafloor

Cass Graybeal Brown, illustrator

The American lobster is easily recognized by two oversized claws on a large, shrimp-like body. Found in rocky reef habitats along the colder coastal waters north of Cape Hatteras, these creatures are one of the world's largest crustaceans. Hiding away during the day, lobsters venture out at night to hunt for fish, crabs, and other invertebrates. Decaying organic matter and algae are also part of their diet. In late summer, American lobsters form long lines and partake in a migration march, single file, into deeper water offshore for the winter. The spiny lobster, a species lacking the enormous claws, occupies similar habitat in the warmer coastal waters south of Cape Hatteras. They also participate in long migration marches into deeper water for the winter.

The heavy claws of the American lobster are different from each other and serve a specialized purpose for acquiring food. The crusher claw, slightly larger with a blunt tooth ridge along the inner edge, can easily crush hard-shelled prey, such as crabs and mollusks. The other claw, with a sharp tooth ridge, is the ripper claw used for tearing and shredding food. Both claws are used for defense, and can inflict significant pain and injury if the lobster is not handled carefully.

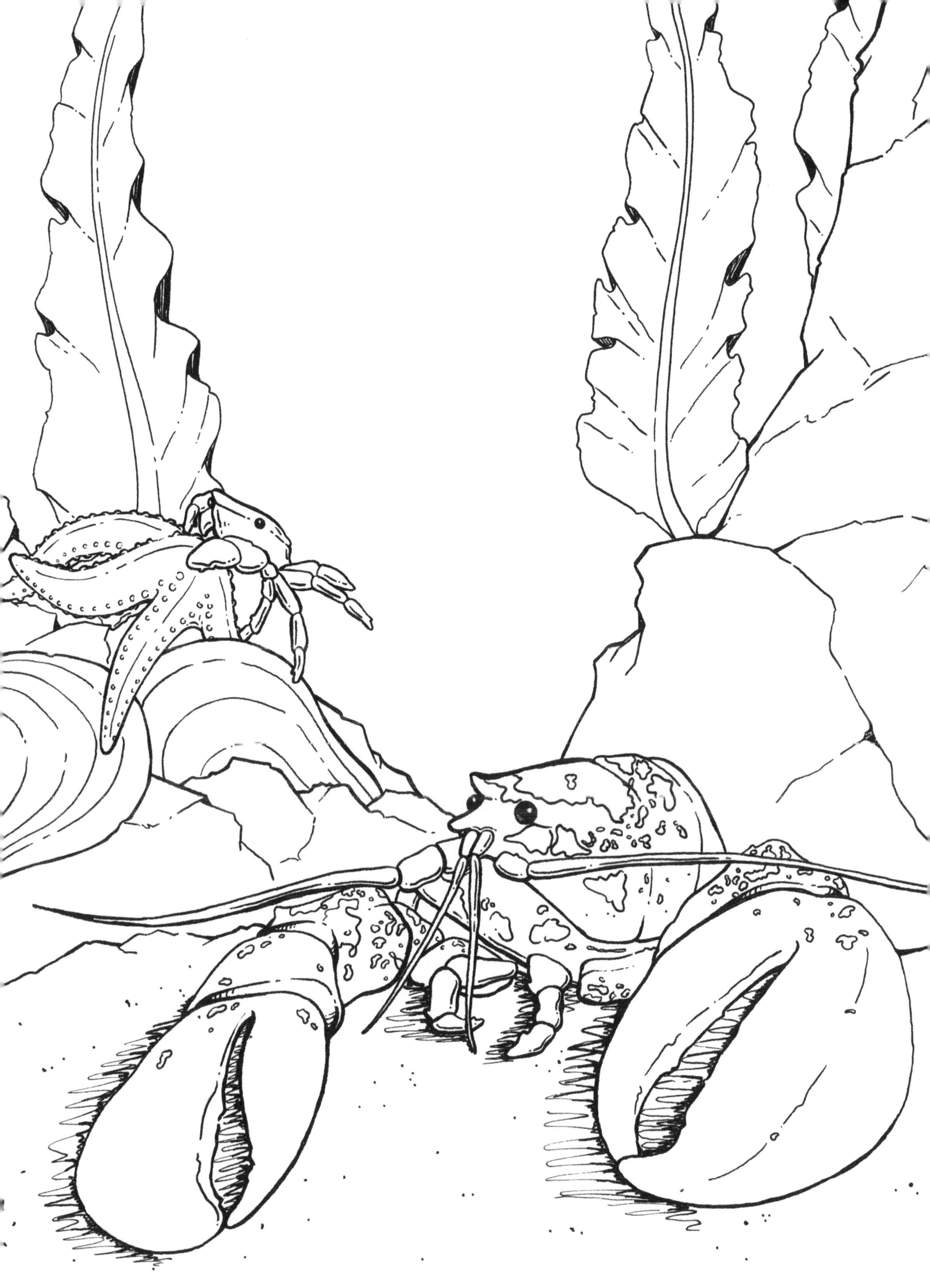

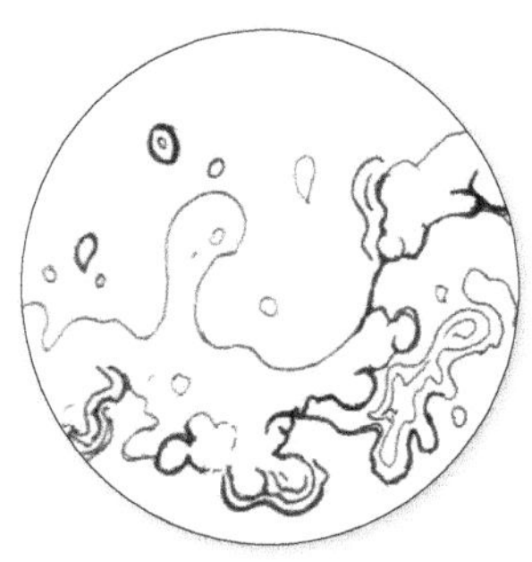

Along the shore

Trenton Jung, illustrator

Along the shore, where the water meets the land, a myriad of life teems in the waves and beneath the sand. Each wave that washes ashore refreshes the activity in the swash zone. Mole crabs and coquina clams burrow, beetles scurry, amphipods and isopods swim, and polychaetes (worms) wriggle between the grains of sand. Life in the swash zone is a struggle against the current and shifting sand to survive. Juvenile fish hang out in the high energy swash zone, feeding on mole crabs and coquinas. Predatory mollusks plow the sandy bottom in a hunt for food. Shorebirds scurry along the receding wave, frantically probing for morsels before the next wave comes rushing ashore. The rhythm of the waves dictates the pace of life along the shore.

Beaches that undergo sand replacement projects are major construction sites. Animals living in the sand along the shore are crushed by the heavy machinery or buried by new sand that is placed on the beach. Many birds and fish species are negatively affected by this loss of life along the water's edge.

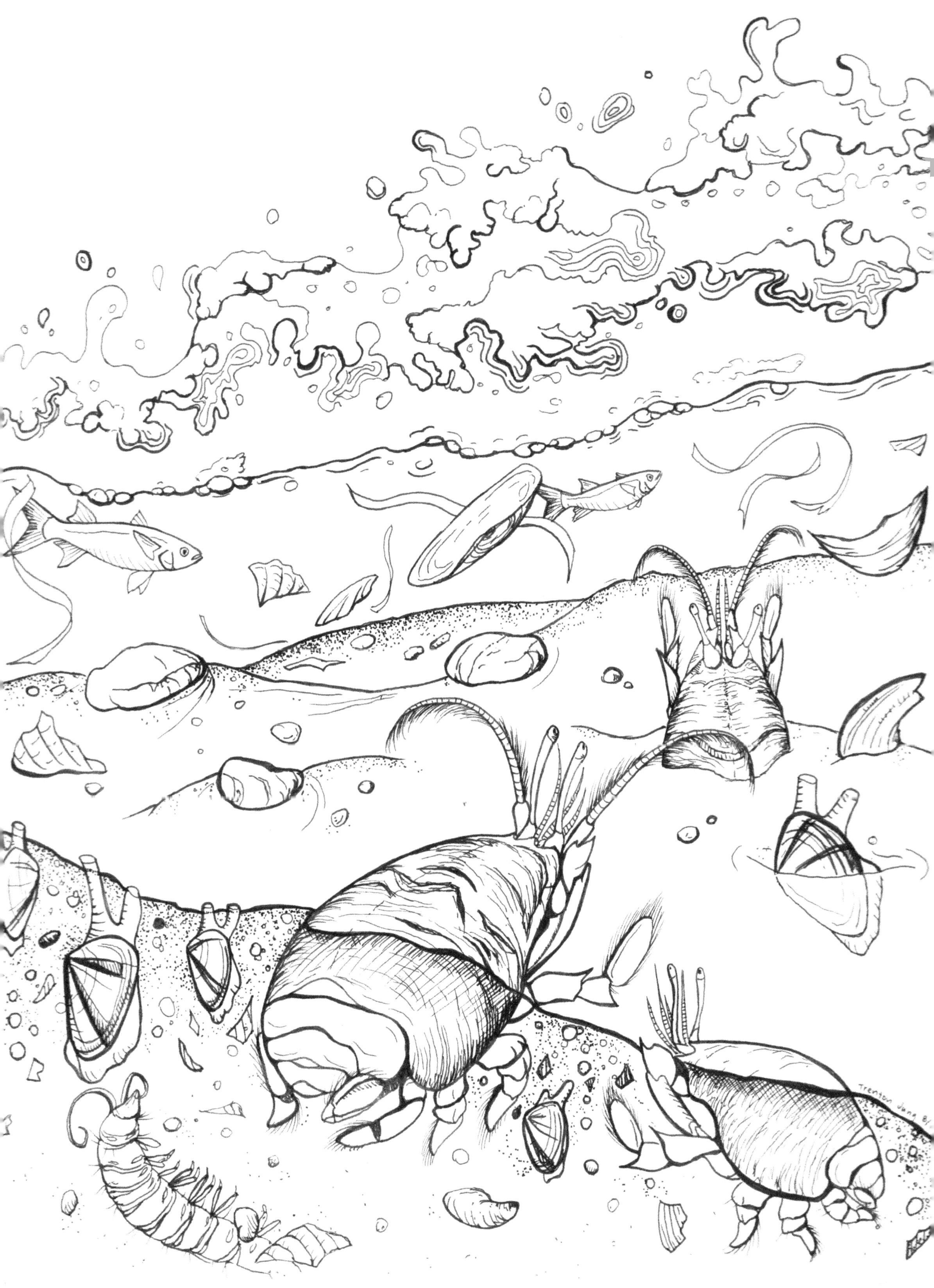
Trenton Jung

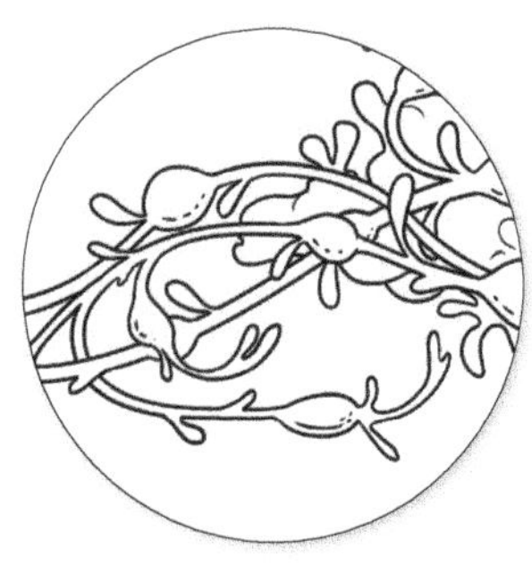

Wrack line

Jennifer Deutscher, illustrator

When the tide recedes after a storm, a wrack line of treasures is left behind on the beach. Matted seaweed and marsh grass may be mixed with an array of hermit crabs in borrowed shells, curlicue egg cases, strange-looking worm casings, and insect-like critters. Imagination can create an explanation for the odds and ends that have washed ashore: a small, rectangular-shaped skate egg case with curly horns can be a mermaid's purse. This tangled organic mess is food and shelter for many shoreline inhabitants. Semipalmated plovers can be seen poking through the mounds looking for insects, worms, and other morsels to eat.

Wrack lines provide important nutrients to the shoreline ecosystem. The mounds of debris also become the foundation of new dunes on the beach by trapping blowing sand.

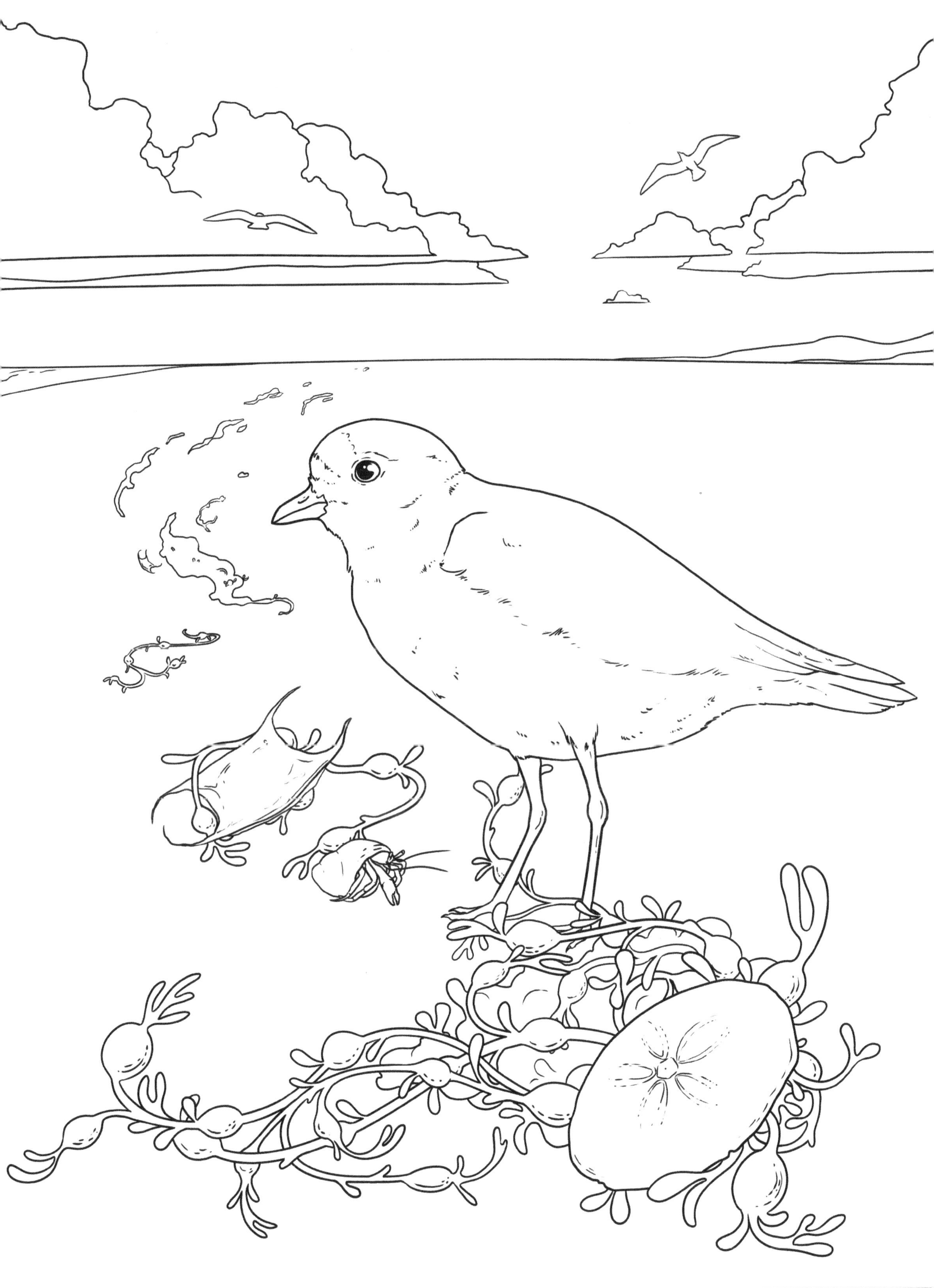

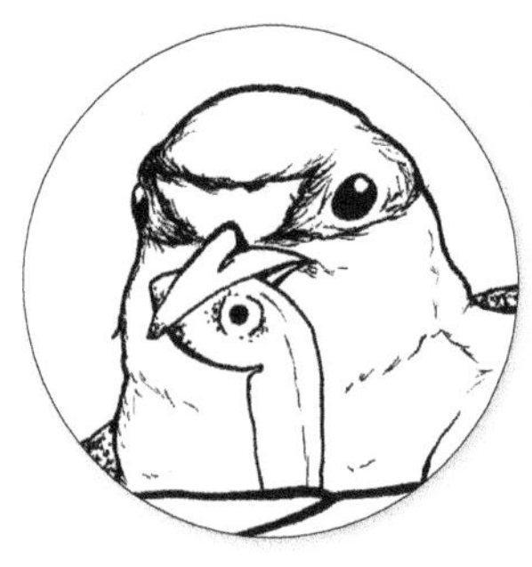

Summer love

Anne Therese J. Namocatcat, illustrator

Terns are small, agile shorebirds with deeply forked tails and straight bills. Hovering about ten feet above the water, terns can detect small fish swimming just below the surface. Terns may gently dip their bills into the water to pluck a fish out or perform a head-first plunge to snag a fish between its bills. During breeding season, the male offers the female a freshly caught fish as a courtship gift. Several hundred terns form a nesting colony along flat, open areas on the beach. Terns aggressively defend the nesting colony, dive-bomb attacking anything they perceive as a threat.

Least terns nest in the same area with other species of terns and skimmers. They all share duties in warding off predators.

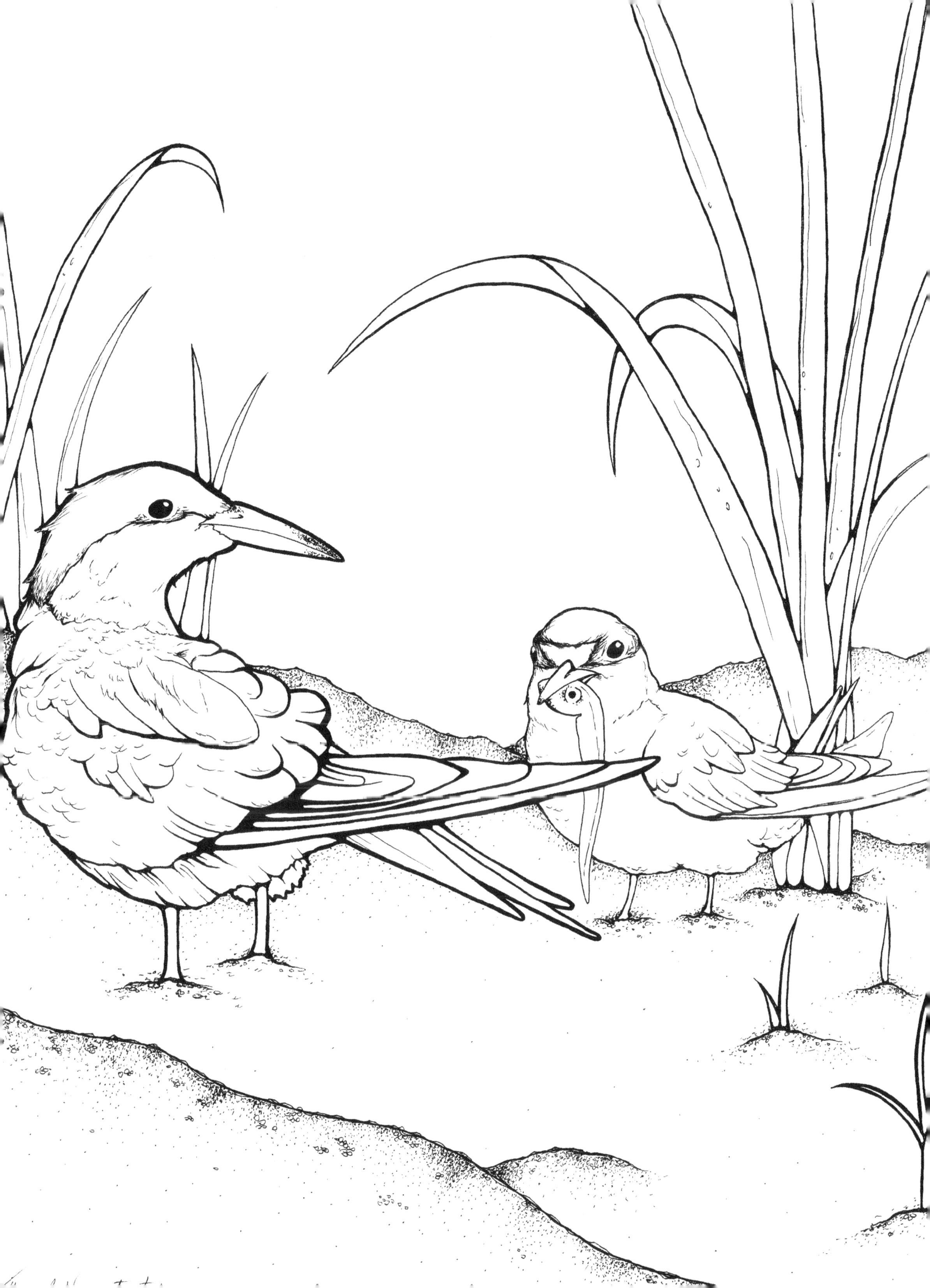

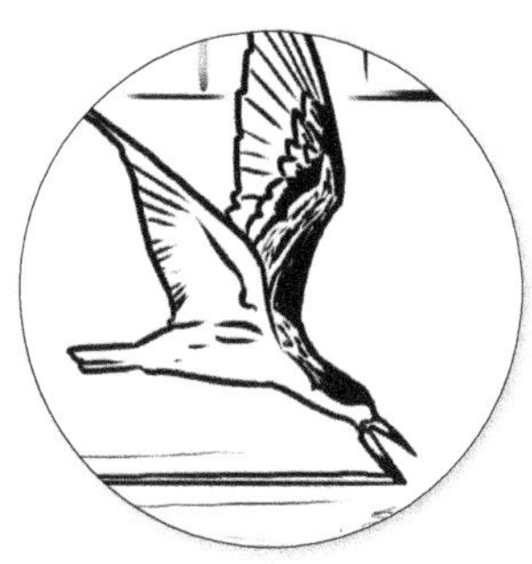

Growing up on the beach

Charon Henning, illustrator

The black skimmer is elegant in flight. With a distinctive black back and hooded mask contrasting with a white belly, the graceful skimmer glides above the water slicing the surface with its lower bill. The lower mandible of this awkward-looking red bill is longer than the upper and sensitive to touch. When the skimming bird detects a fish against its bill, it snaps the upper bill closed with a downward head jerk. Skimmers nest on the ground on open sandy beaches in secluded areas. The nest is a small scrape in the sand with three to six eggs. Both male and female tend to the eggs and raise the hatchlings.

On a hot summer day, sand can heat up to 140°F. Nesting birds on the beach, like the black skimmers, provide shade over the nest to keep the eggs from overheating. If the parent bird is frightened off the nest, sand temperature becomes dangerously hot in a short time and the developing chick inside the egg will die.

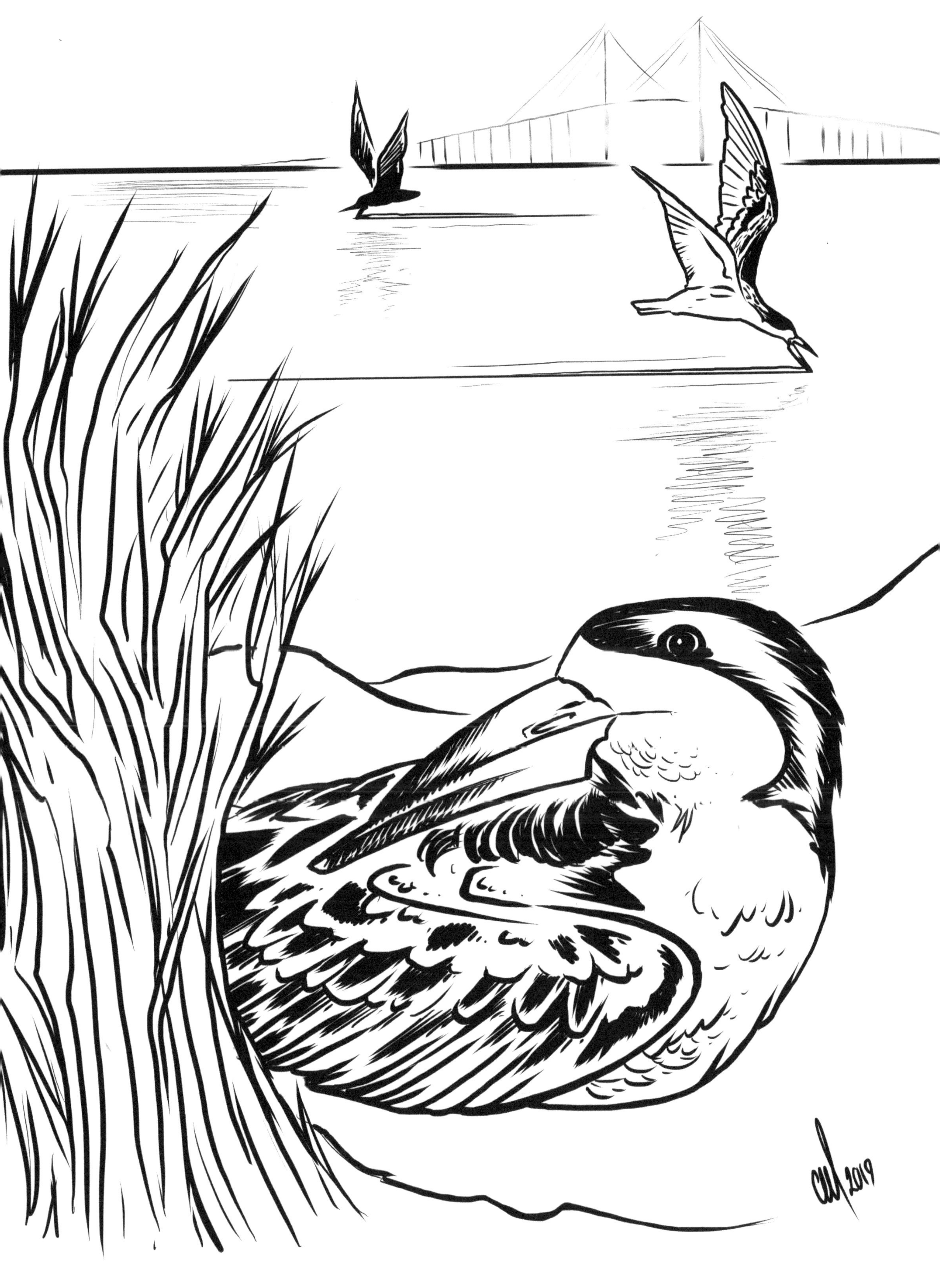

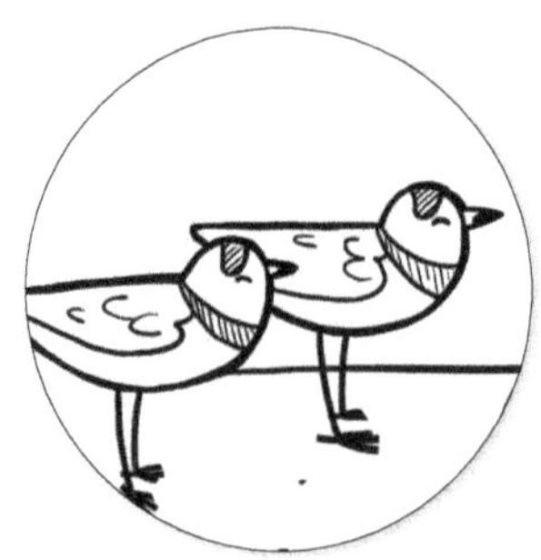

Blending with the sand

Clara Hunt, illustrator

It's hard to hide on a flat sandy beach, but piping plovers do a good job. These small birds with sand gray backs can hide in plain sight, blending into the background of sandy beach shores. Piping plovers scurry in quick bursts along the drier portion of the beach, along the water's edge, or on the muddy tidal flats. These petite plovers perform a shuffle dance while foraging.

Holes in the beach are often the first clue that ghost crabs are present. Ghost crabs blend in so well with the sand that they often go undetected until they make a mad dash across the beach. These crabs usually inhabit the upper, drier portion of the beach. Entry holes will lead to an underground chamber, perhaps several feet down, where a crab spends time hiding. Several tunnels can lead to the same chamber. Though more active at night, ghost crabs will venture out of their burrow during the day. They are opportunistic scavengers, and will eat almost any organic matter that washes in with the tide. They also have an appetite for sea turtle eggs, sea turtle hatchlings, and shorebird chicks.

Ghost crabs have gills, but spend most of the time on the land or in a burrow. In order to pull oxygen out of the air, ghost crabs must keep their gills wet. Several times a day, ghost crabs make a dash into the water to replenish the moisture on the gills. If their gills dry out, the crabs will suffocate. However, if the crabs spend too much time in the water, they will drown.

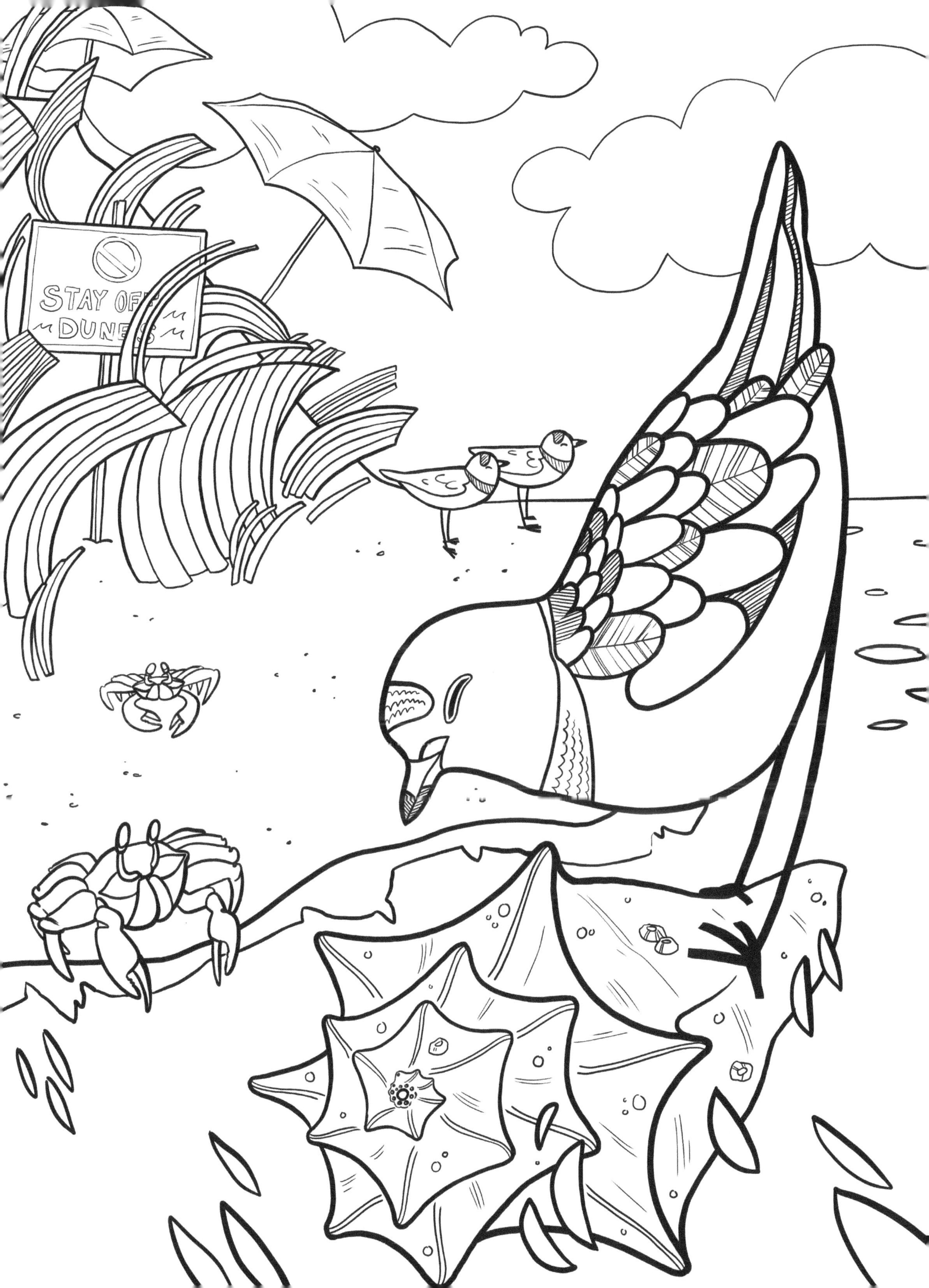
STAY OFF
DUNES

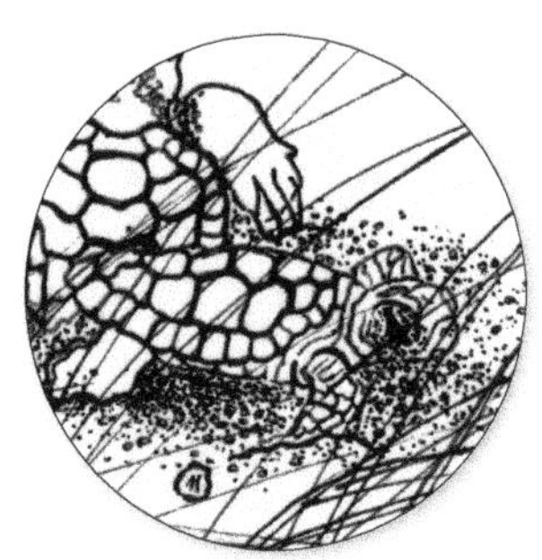

Beach beginnings

Cordelia Norris, illustrator

Loggerheads are the most common sea turtle to nest along the Atlantic coast. Under the cover of darkness, the female emerges from the ocean and lumbers onto the beach. Using her rear flippers, she scoops out a narrow cavity in a spot high on the beach near the base of the dunes. After depositing around 130 ping pong ball size eggs, she covers everything, flings sand around to camouflage the location, and then returns to the sea. The unattended nest is vulnerable to predation by foxes, coyotes, raccoons, and ghost crabs. About 60 days later, the eggs begin to hatch, but the baby turtles wait inside the nest. Typically at night, the surface of the sand begins to boil as a mass of palm-sized hatchlings climbs out of the nest cavity. Flippers frantically flapping, they make a mad dash to the ocean, racing against hungry gulls and ghost crabs. Once in the ocean, the turtles swim for their life. If lucky, the hatchlings will elude predators, and reach the safety of Sargassum seaweed mats in the open ocean. Loggerheads return to inshore waters when they reach about 18 inches in length. They stay along the coast, migrating to warmer water with the seasons. It may take 30 years for loggerhead turtles to become adults. They spend almost their entire life in the ocean, with only the females venturing back on land to nest.

The sand temperature surrounding the eggs in a sea turtle nest determines whether the hatchlings will be mostly males or females. Higher nest temperatures result in more females, while cooler temperatures produce more males.

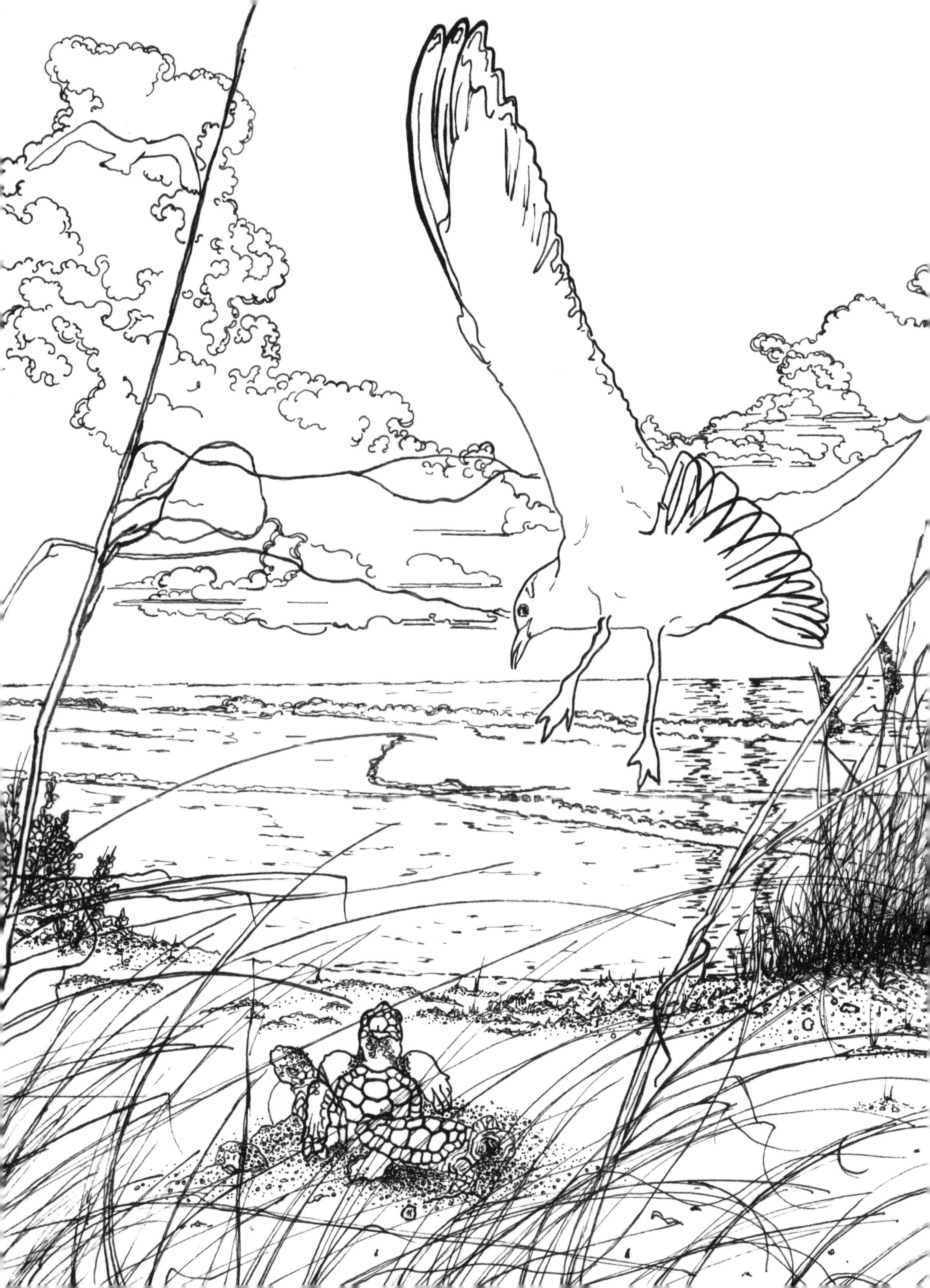

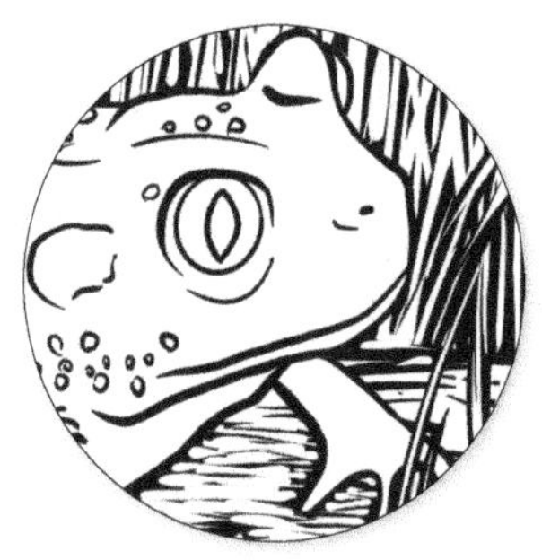

Between the dunes

Carrie Carlson, illustrator

Behind the ocean-facing primary dunes, low sandy areas stretch between rows of dune ridges. Moist grasslands and dense shrubs cover the area away from the ocean, gradually blending into maritime forest. Sawgrass, black needlerush, and salt meadow hay are a few of the grasses that can establish a root-hold in the sandy swale. Shrubs, such as wax myrtle and Yaupon holly, provide protective cover for animals in the swale ecosystem. The Eastern spadefoot toad lives most of its life in underground burrows throughout the sandy soil swales. When heavy rains create temporary freshwater ponds, the toad emerges to breed. Eggs are attached to underwater vegetation. The tadpoles hatch in about ten days, and grow into toads within four to six weeks. The new Eastern spadefoot toads must be fully grown before the water disappears.

Interdunal swales on barrier islands are susceptible to salt water inundation during extreme high tides and storms. Waves from the ocean push over the dunes, creating overwash areas. Plants are buried with sand and the area is flattened. Exotic and invasive plant species that are salt-tolerant, such as beach vitex and phragmites, can move into the overwash areas and compete with the weakened native plants. Invasive plants choke out native plants, making survival difficult for the animals that depend on the native species.

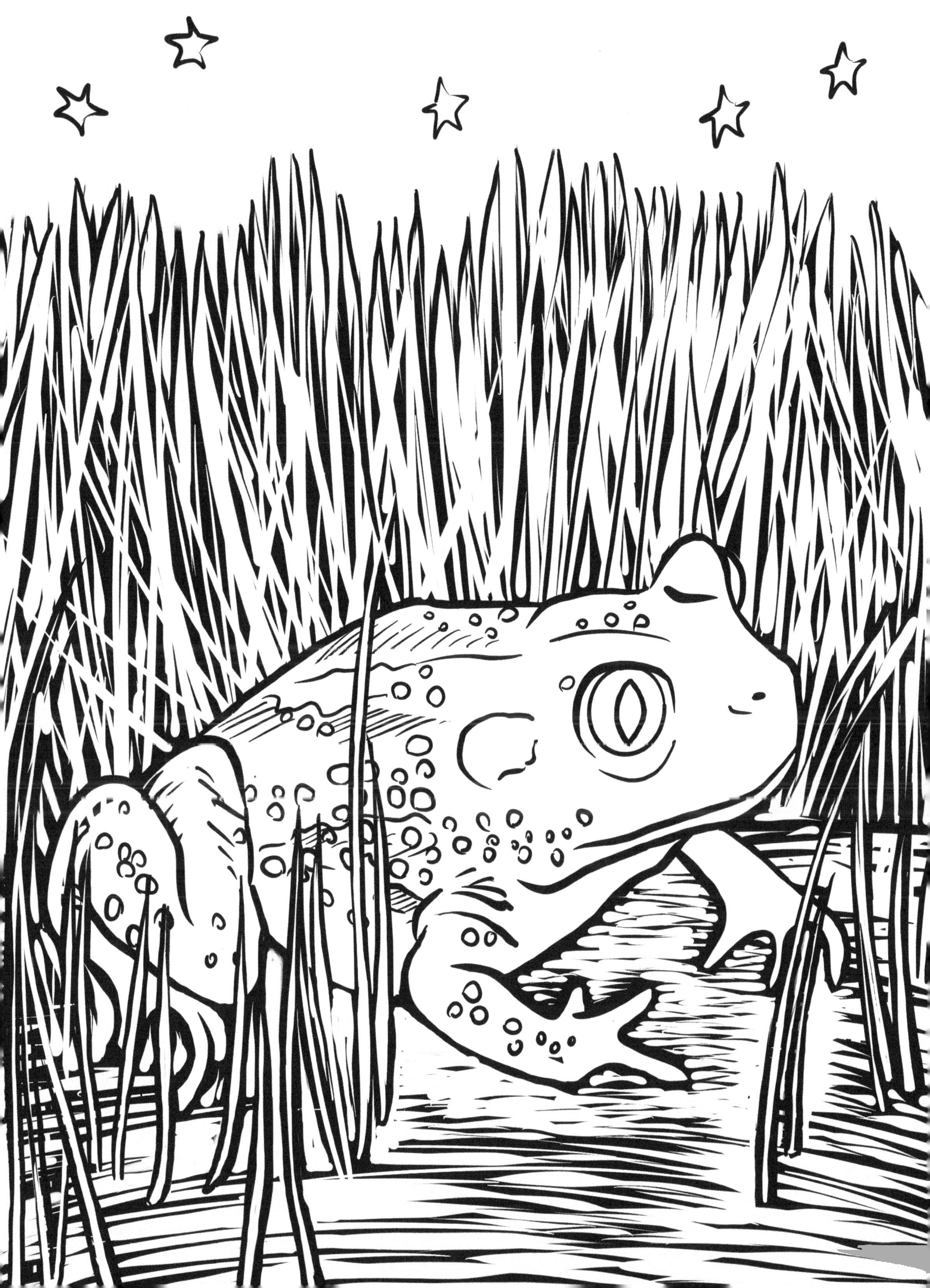

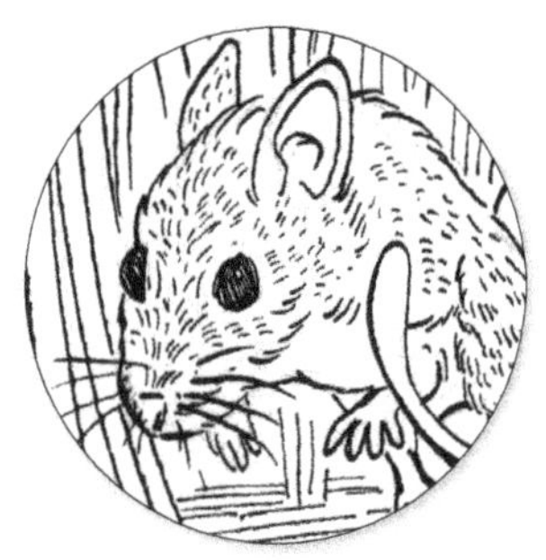

Hidden among the reeds

Zach Schrange, illustrator

Flying low over the grassy upland marsh and swales, a Northern harrier is scanning for movement on the ground. The hawk is a natural predator of small rodents found in the upland marsh and swale ecosystems. Keen hearing allows this hawk to detect small animals hiding among the grasses and shrubs. Tiny rodents, like beach mice, use the protective cover the swales provide while seeking seeds, fruits, and insects to eat. However, these small animals are threatened by habitat fragmentation caused by coastal property development, which seriously impacts their ability to survive, putting the hawk's food source at risk.

Northern harriers, also known as marsh hawks, spend the winter along the East Coast. They are the only harrier species found in North America.

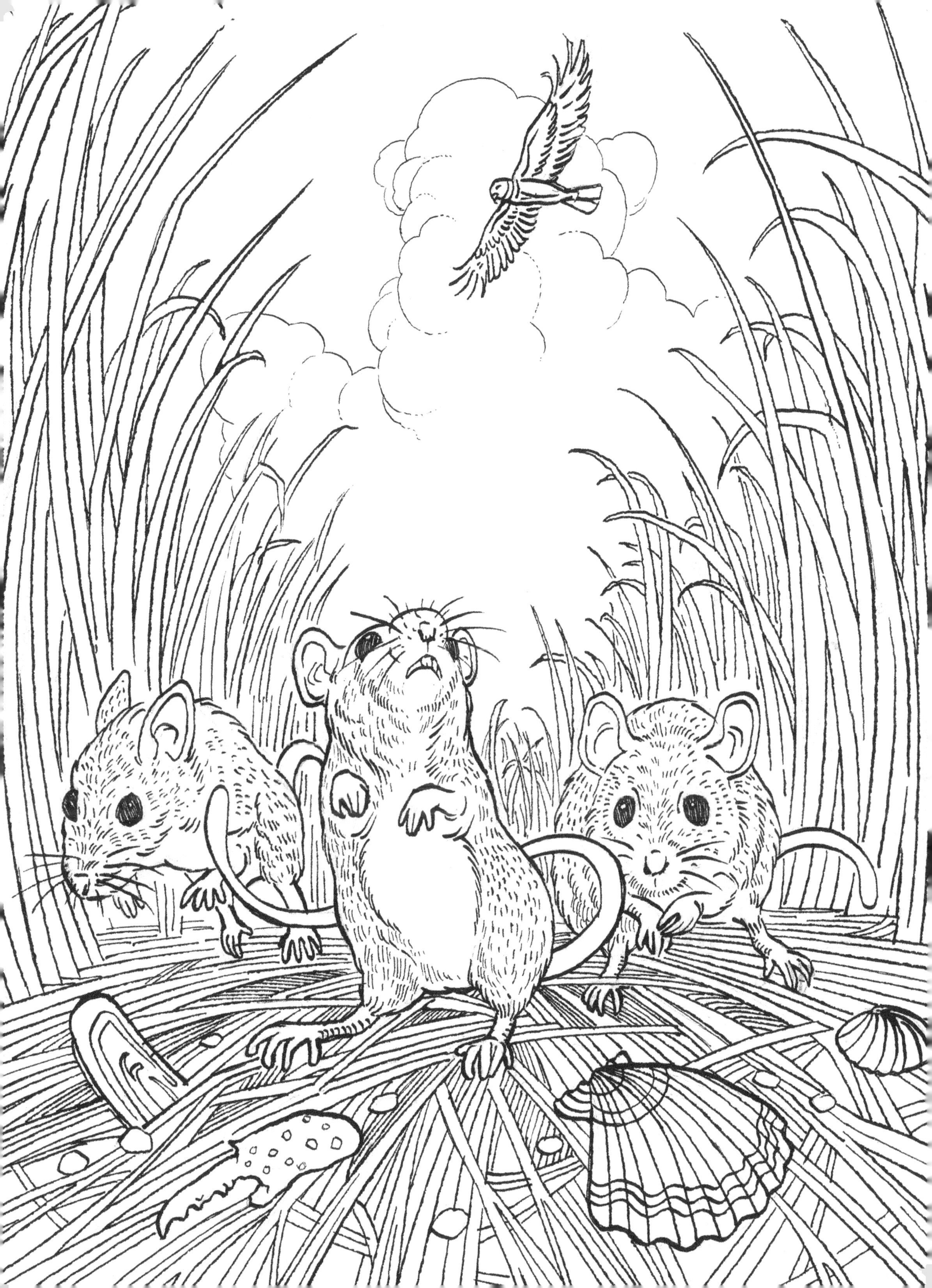

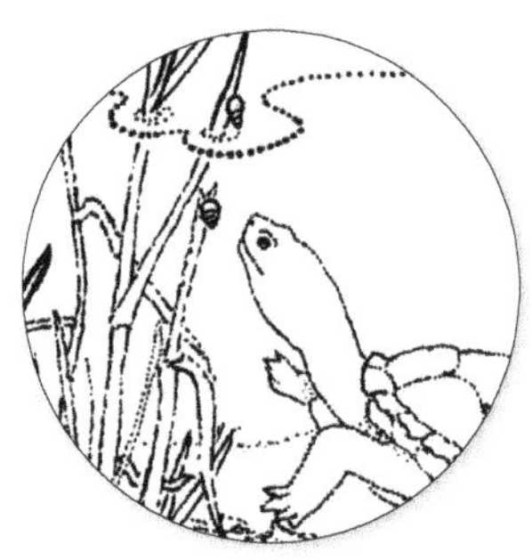

Tidal salt marsh

Anne Runyon, illustrator

Brackish water flows through the estuaries. The fringes of the estuary flood and ebb along the shoreline with the changing tide, creating the salt marsh ecosystem. The North American east coast experiences two tidal cycles each day. The water level is constantly changing. High tide brings salty water from the ocean into the estuary. As the tide recedes, fresh water from rivers and streams dilute the salt water. Juvenile fish, diamondback terrapins, blue crabs, and horseshoe crabs follow the water flow in and out of the salt marsh. Periwinkle snails prefer to stay above the water, climbing up and down the marsh grass as the water rises and falls. Oysters and barnacles open when the tide is in, but close tight when the tide is out. Mud flats are flooded at high tide and exposed at low tide. The animals either move with the water, close up tight, or come out into the air when the water leaves. The life cycles in the salt marsh follow the movement of the tide.

The gravitational pull from the moon causes the daily tidal change on Earth. Wind and weather patterns also affect the height of each tide. Winds blowing onshore and strong storms tend to push more water landward, causing higher-than-normal tides. Strong offshore winds will keep water from moving ashore, resulting in lower low tides.

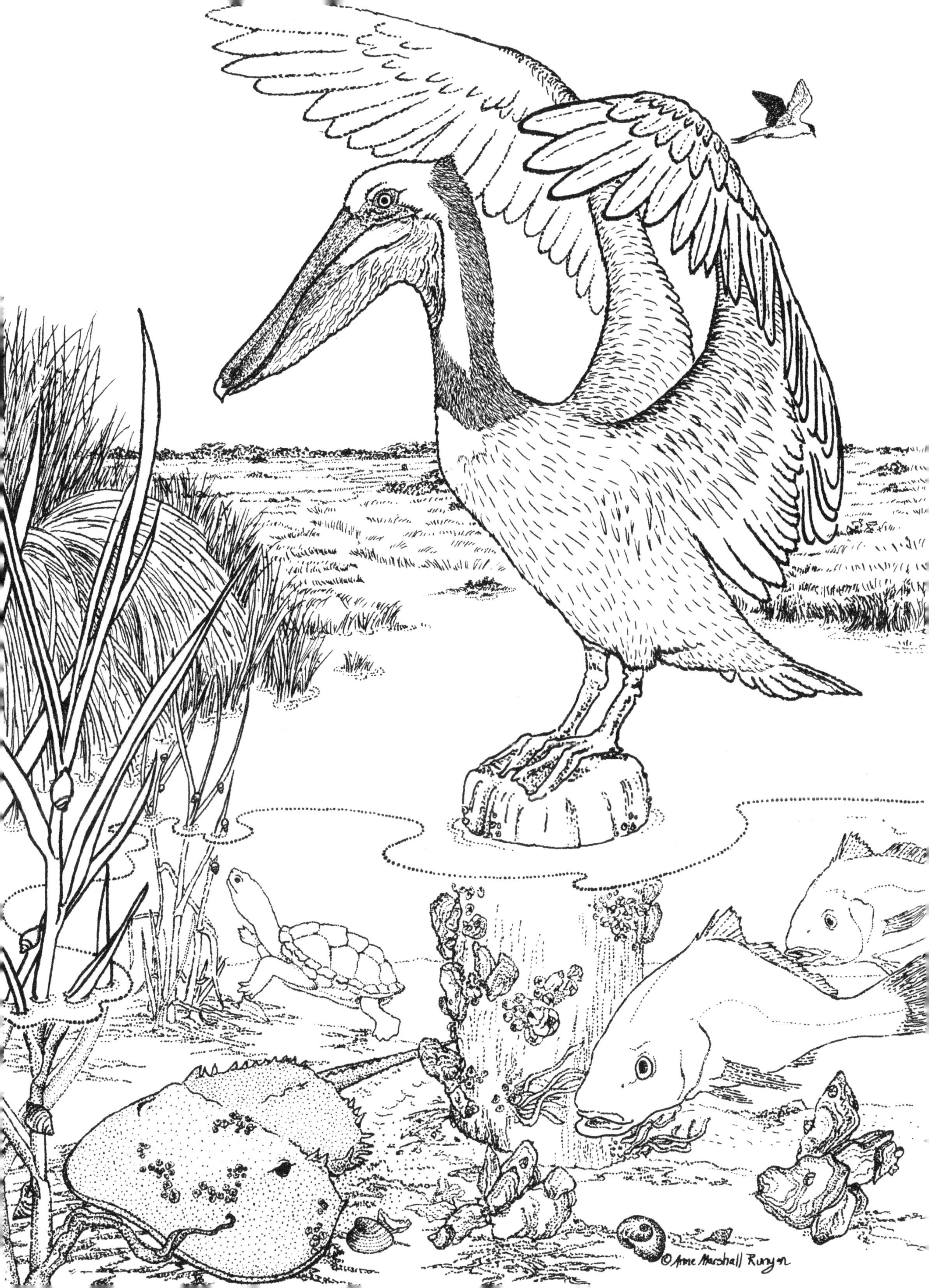
©Anne Marshall Runyon

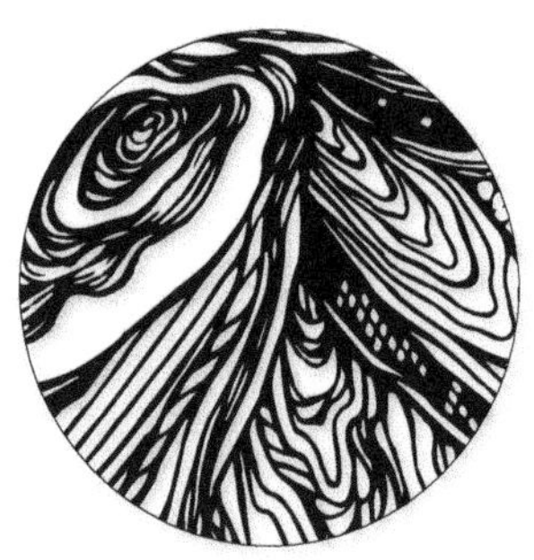

Salt marsh engineers

Heather Divoky, illustrator

Oysters cement themselves to one another to form large communities of several thousand individuals in shallow estuary waters. These reefs can be left high and dry at low tide, but the oysters are tightly sealed within their shells waiting for the water to cover them again. Oysters are considered estuary engineers with important responsibilities: constructing habitats, creating storm barriers, improving water quality, and providing food. Oyster reefs provide habitats for over 300 different species of animals, including fish, shrimp, crabs, worms, and other mollusks. A natural barrier is created by oyster reefs, absorbing wave energy. The barrier protects coastal plants and reduces erosion along the shoreline. Oysters have a valuable role in the estuary as biological filters. One oyster can filter 50 gallons of water a day. The oyster population in Chesapeake Bay during the early 1900s could filter the entire volume of Bay water every three to four days. Now, the current number of oysters in the Bay would require about a year to accomplish the same feat. Oysters are also an important food source for a variety of fish, birds, crabs, other mollusks, as well as people.

"He was a bold man that first ate an oyster." — Jonathan Swift

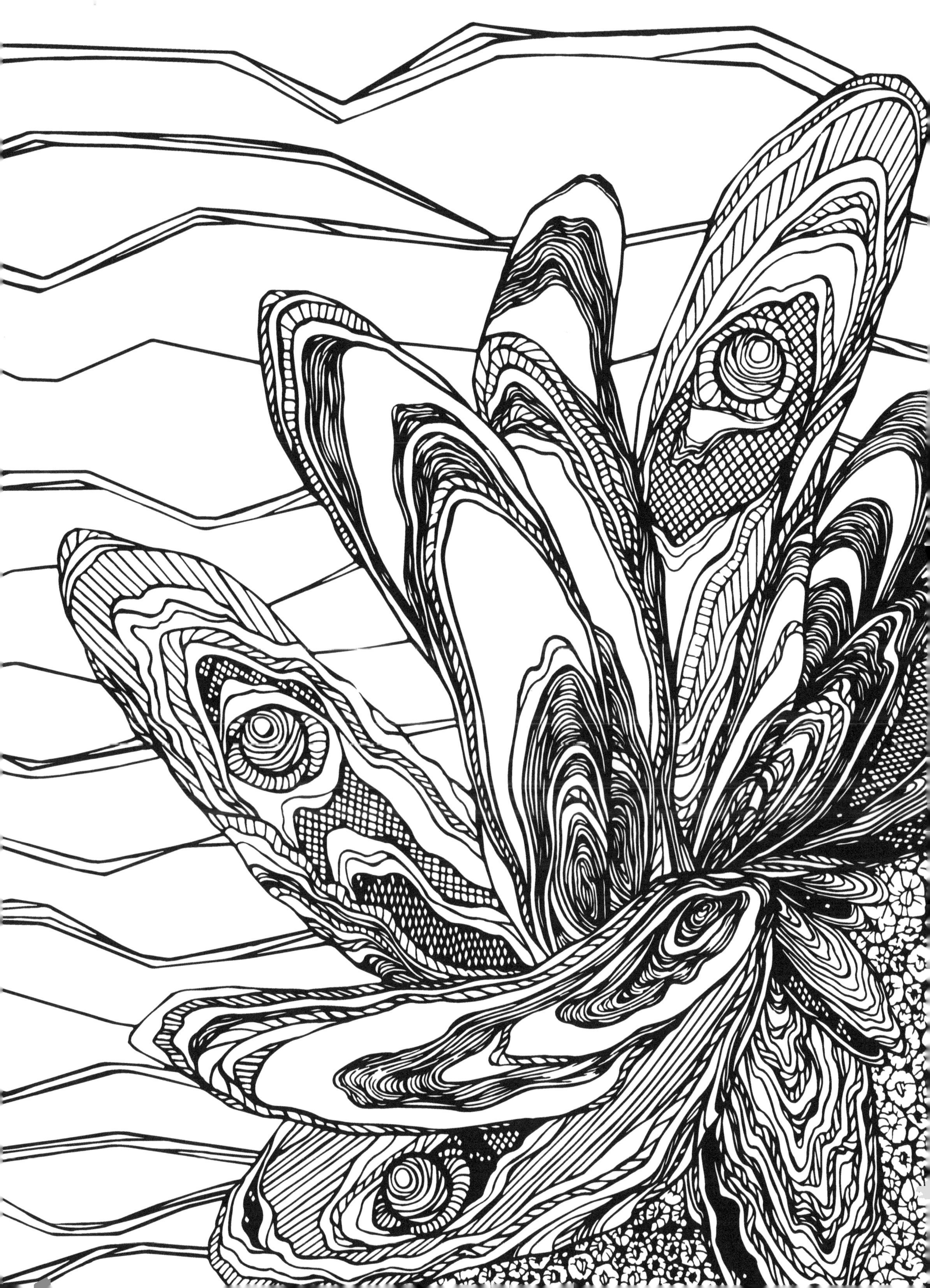

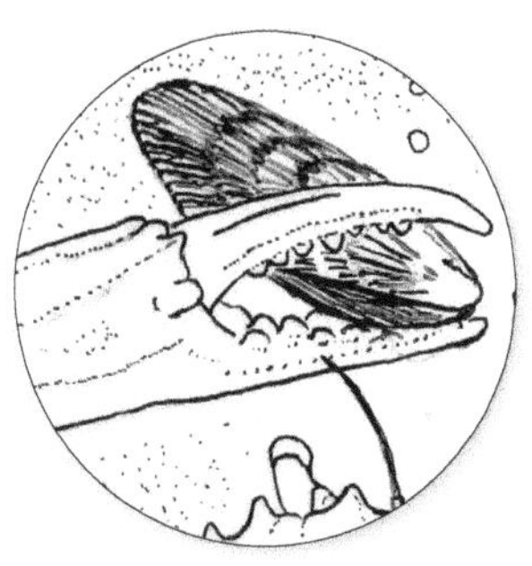

Beauty in the estuary

Lucy Gagliardo, illustrator

The Atlantic blue crab is a culinary delicacy. The scientific name, *Callinectes sapidus*, means savory, beautiful swimmer. The blue crab is an important inhabitant of the brackish estuaries along the North American Atlantic coast. As an opportunistic feeder, it doesn't matter to the blue crab if the food is dead or alive. Blue crabs feast on fish and shrimp, rounding out its diet with clams, mussels, seaweed and other algae, and even other crabs. The dark olive-green carapace contrasts with its royal blue claws. The female's claws are tipped with red. The blue crab spends most of its life in the estuary, preferring the brackish water. However, the female blue crab must migrate to the ocean to release her eggs into saltier water. The tiny blue crab larva begins its life as microscopic zooplankton in the ocean. It grows, molts, and changes into a second stage that gradually finds its way back into the estuary. Once there, it finally changes into a juvenile crab about the size of a pinhead. A female blue crab can produce up to eight million eggs, but only about one in a million will survive to adulthood.

The sex of a blue crab can be identified by the apron shape on its underbelly. An immature female crab has a triangular-shaped apron, and a mature female has a rounded, dome-shaped apron. The apron on a male is a thin pencil shape. The immature female is called a Sally, and the mature female is a Sook. The male crab is a Jimmy.

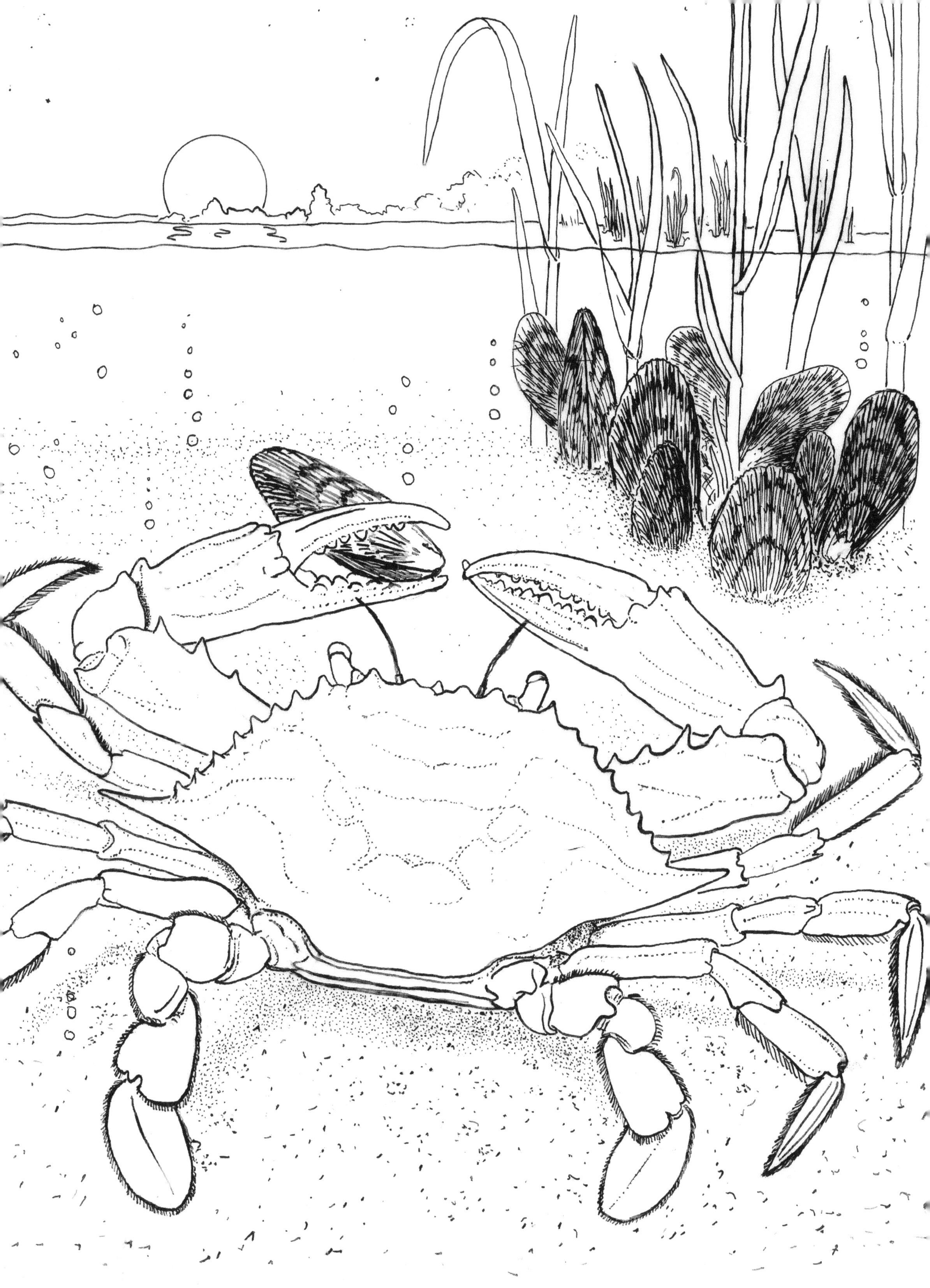

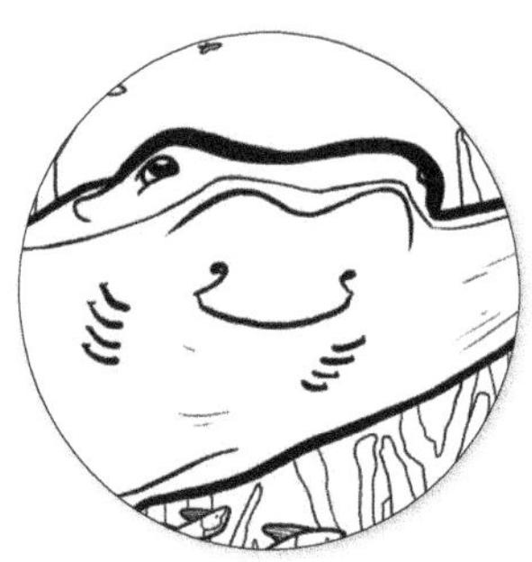

Estuary nursery

Clara Hunt, illustrator

Estuary water is not as salty as the ocean. Fresh water from rivers, streams, and creeks mix with salty ocean water to create brackish water. Brackish water provides ideal nursery conditions for many aquatic species in the estuary. Eggs can develop and hatch, while juveniles are able to grow and mature. Submerged reeds and grasses, even discarded shells, are ideal shelters for young fish, shrimp, cownose rays, and other species. Chesapeake Bay is a large nursery area for cownose rays. Every spring, thousands of cownose rays migrate into the Bay. The females give birth to one pup and then mate again. The rays stay in the Bay throughout the summer months. Adult males leave in late summer, while the females stay until September or mid-October. Cownose rays migrate along the East Coast, spending the winter months off the Florida coast. It is uncertain where the newborn and yearlings spend their first couple of years, but within two to four years, the juveniles return to the Bay in the spring along with the older adults.

Scientific research indicates that over 90% of commercially valuable seafood depend on the marsh-estuary ecosystems at some point in their lives. Ocean-Spawned, Estuarine-Nursery Dependent (OSEND) species include shrimp and crabs, menhaden and mullet, and many other species of fish. Estuaries provide OSEND species plentiful food to eat and protective cover to escape predators.

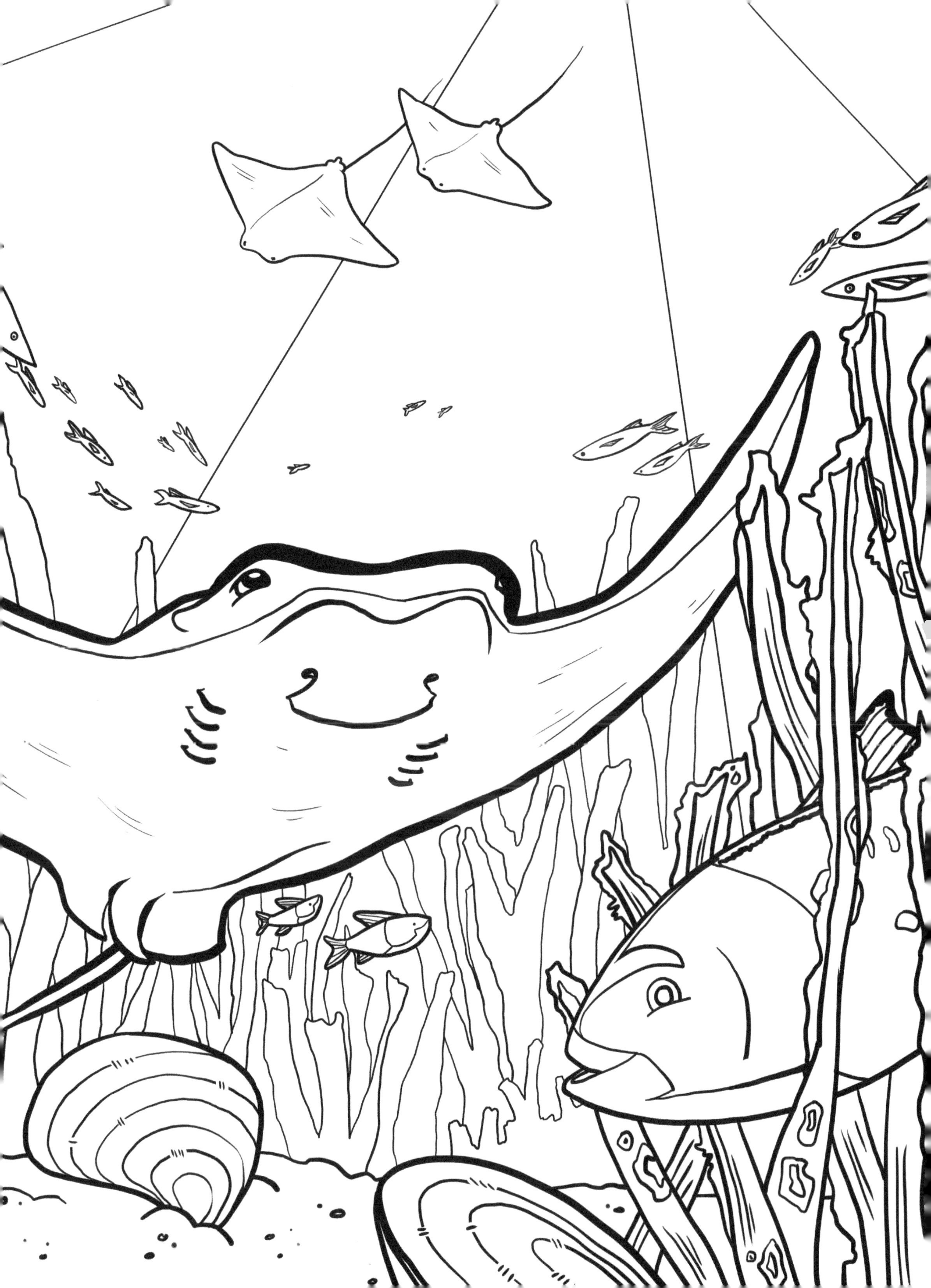

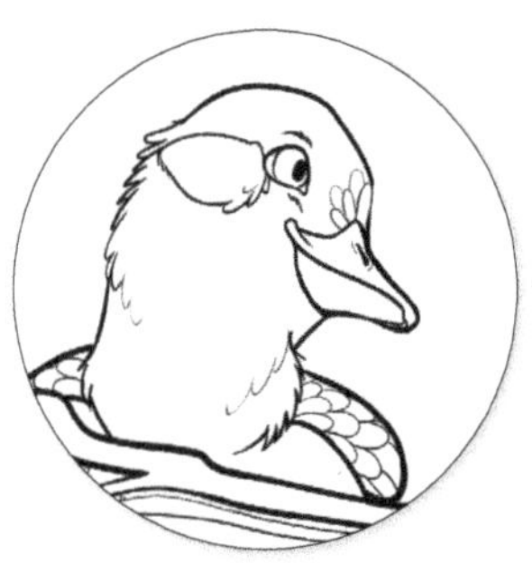

Winter vacation

Sami Hernandez, illustrator

Buffleheads, the smallest of the diving ducks, are common winter visitors along the East Coast. Flying from their summer breeding grounds in Alaska and northern Canada, buffleheads find saltwater bays along the coast to their liking. They are usually seen in pairs, sometimes together in small groups. At least one bufflehead in the group will stay atop the water to keep watch while the others are diving. The duck will stay submerged for 12-25 seconds while scouring up shrimp, small crabs, snails, and other aquatic invertebrates before bobbing to the surface like a cork. Buffleheads are constantly moving, either swimming along on the water's surface or diving underneath in search of food. They rarely come ashore. Unlike other ducks that must run along the water's surface to launch into flight, buffleheads can take off straight up into the air.

The ocean acts like a giant solar panel absorbing heat from the sun. The release of the ocean's heat into the atmosphere regulates the air temperatures along the coast. In the summer, temperatures stay noticeably cooler along the coast than just a few miles inland; in the winter, temperatures will be warmer.

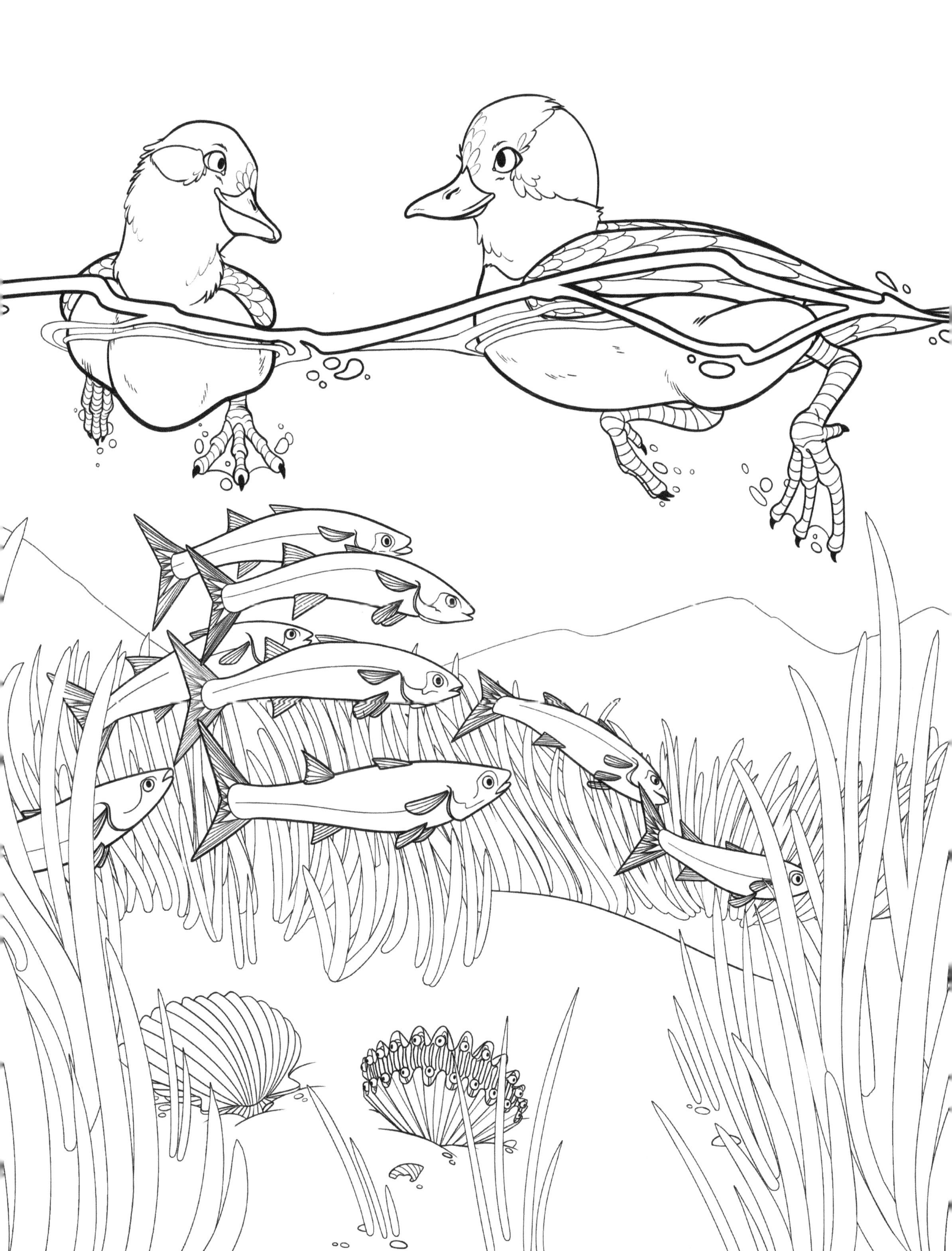

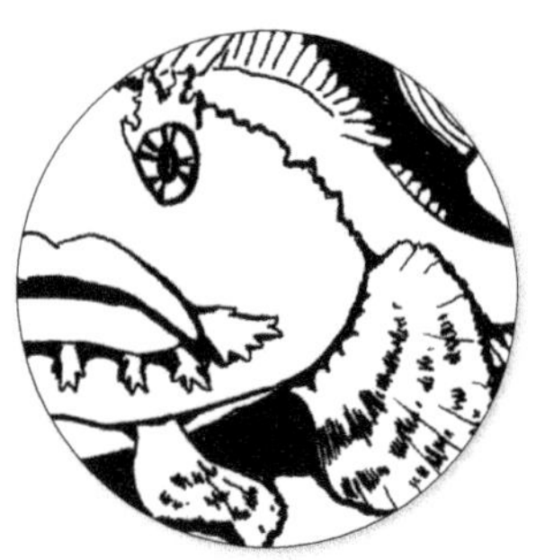

Hidden in the rubble

Jennifer Landin, illustrator

Perfectly camouflaged in a pile of discarded shells, a hidden oyster toadfish uses its two big bulging eyes to scan for unsuspecting shrimp or fish. With a tremendous mouth, the toadfish is quick to ambush its prey. Grotesque flaps hanging from various parts of its body and hidden venomous spines keep most predators away. Because its inner ear system is similar to humans, the oyster toadfish was on board several space shuttle missions as part of research studying microgravity effects in adapting to weightlessness.

The horseshoe crab is an arthropod, more closely related to spiders and scorpions and not a true crab. Fossil records show the horseshoe crab was in the oceans hundreds of million years before the dinosaurs existed on land. With ten eyes and blue blood, the horseshoe crab is an important resource for scientific research and medical testing. Their eyes have provided insight into the working of human vision. A type of immune cell in the blood causes quick clotting in the presence of bacterial toxins, making it a crucial component in testing for contamination in the manufacturing of drugs and medical equipment. Research efforts to replicate this immune cell may eliminate the need to capture and draw blood from these prehistoric creatures.

The polychaete clam worm has four eyes, jaw-like pincers on its head, and pairs of appendages sticking out from each body segment. This alien-looking worm is probably the most abundant polychaete in the estuaries. It is a valuable food source for many bottom-dwelling animals, including horseshoe crabs and oyster toadfish.

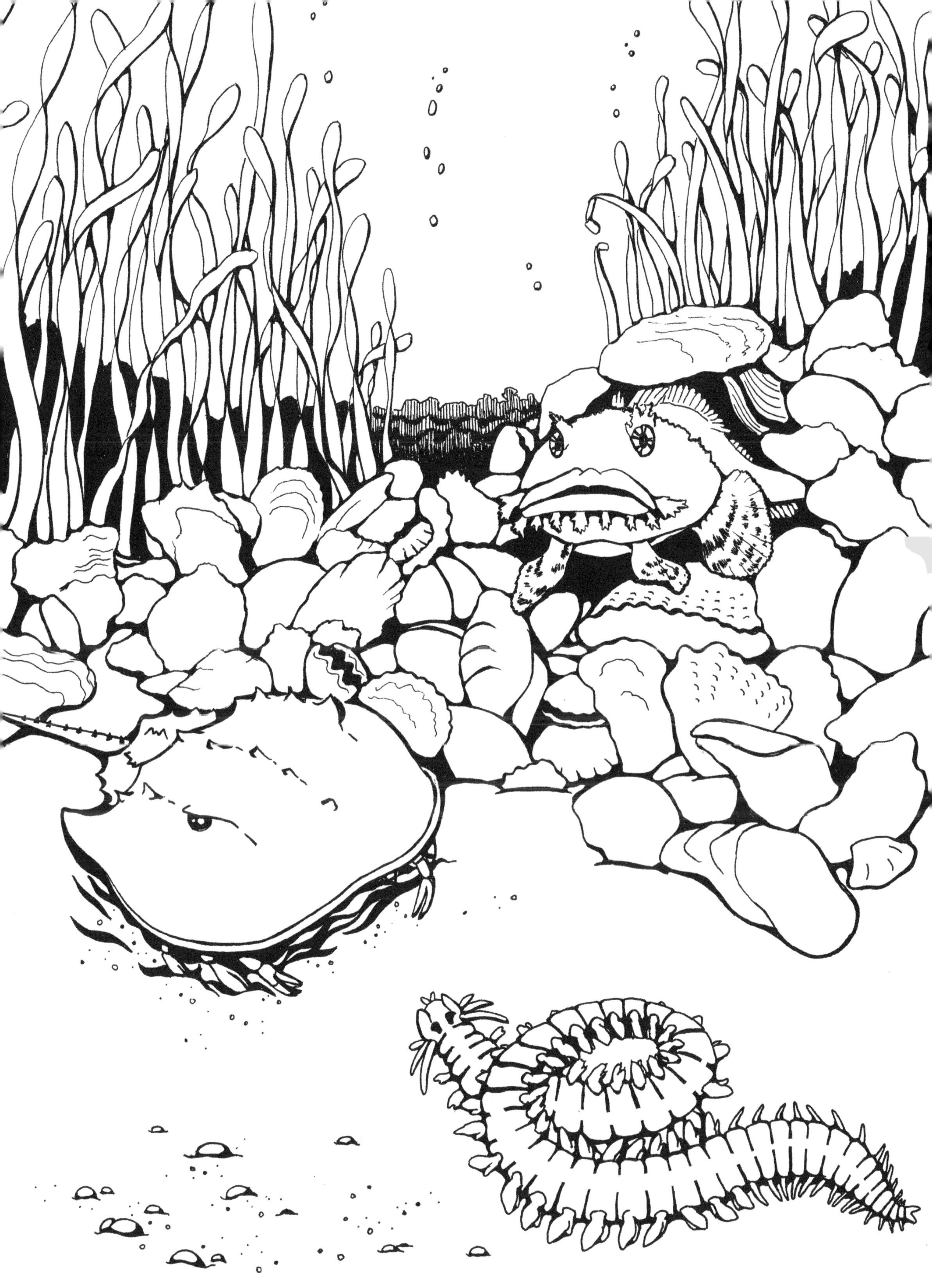

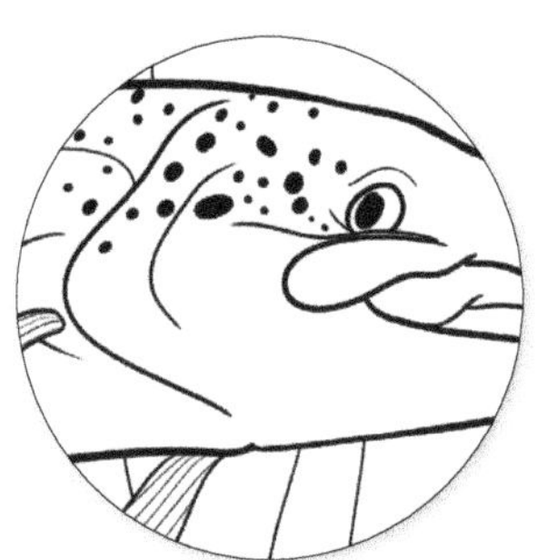

From the river to the sea

Sami Hernandez, illustrator

The Atlantic salmon is one of the largest-sized salmon species in the world. Once common in every river north of the Hudson River, the last of the wild Atlantic salmon now are found only in about eight rivers in Maine. Atlantic salmon are anadromous: they begin their life cycle in freshwater rivers and migrate to the ocean where most of their adult life is spent. When it is time to spawn, the salmon will return to freshwater rivers. Unlike Pacific salmon, Atlantic salmon do not die after spawning. Instead, they head to the ocean to recover and live for several years before returning to the rivers to spawn.

All Atlantic salmon sold in the United States is farm-raised and commercially grown. The remaining wild populations of Atlantic salmon in the Gulf of Maine are protected by the Endangered Species Act. It is illegal to commercially or recreationally catch wild Atlantic salmon.

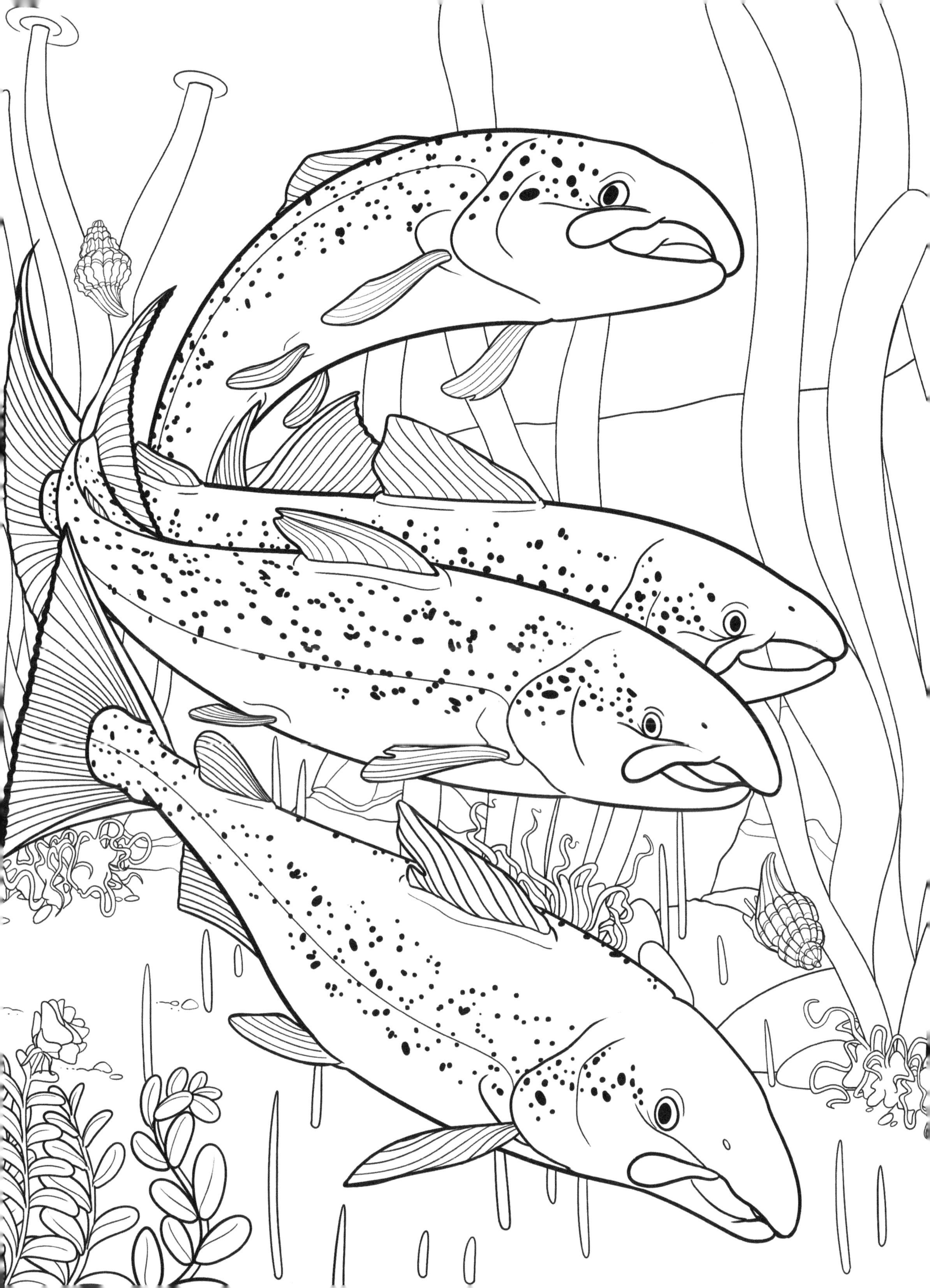

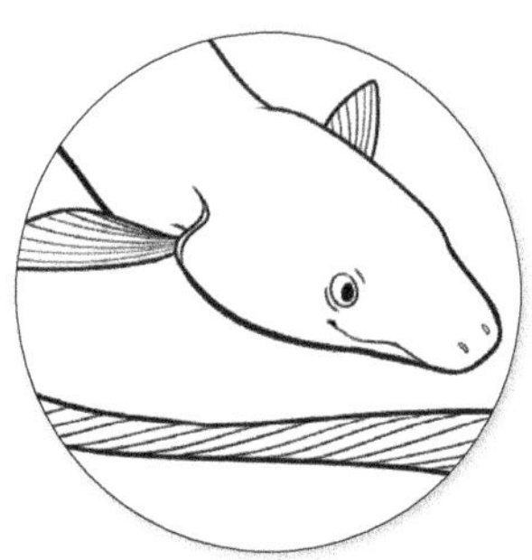

From the sea to the river

Sami Hernandez, illustrator

The American eel is a peculiar-looking fish resembling a snake without scales. These eels are catadromous, meaning they are freshwater fish that migrate to the ocean to spawn. Their lifecycle is complex: They begin life in a larval stage that looks like a transparent willow leaf, and spend about a year riding the ocean currents toward the North American coast from the Sargasso Sea. The larvae grow into clear worm-like glass eels called elvers, and make their way into the coastal area. Once reaching the estuaries, they develop a dark greenish-brown pigment and continue the journey into freshwater rivers and streams. The females travel far upriver, while the males tend to stay near the estuaries. Having traveled perhaps more than a thousand miles, the elvers change into yellow eels. For the next six to thirty years, the eels will live in fresh or brackish waters eating snails and other mollusks, small crabs and other crustaceans, worms, and small fish. Metamorphosing one more time into sexually mature silver eels, they embark on the long marathon swim back to the Sargasso Sea, where they spawn and die.

American eels sometimes swim onto the land to get around barricades in the river. When out of the water, eels secrete a slimy mucous, making them extremely slippery so they can slide easily along the river banks.

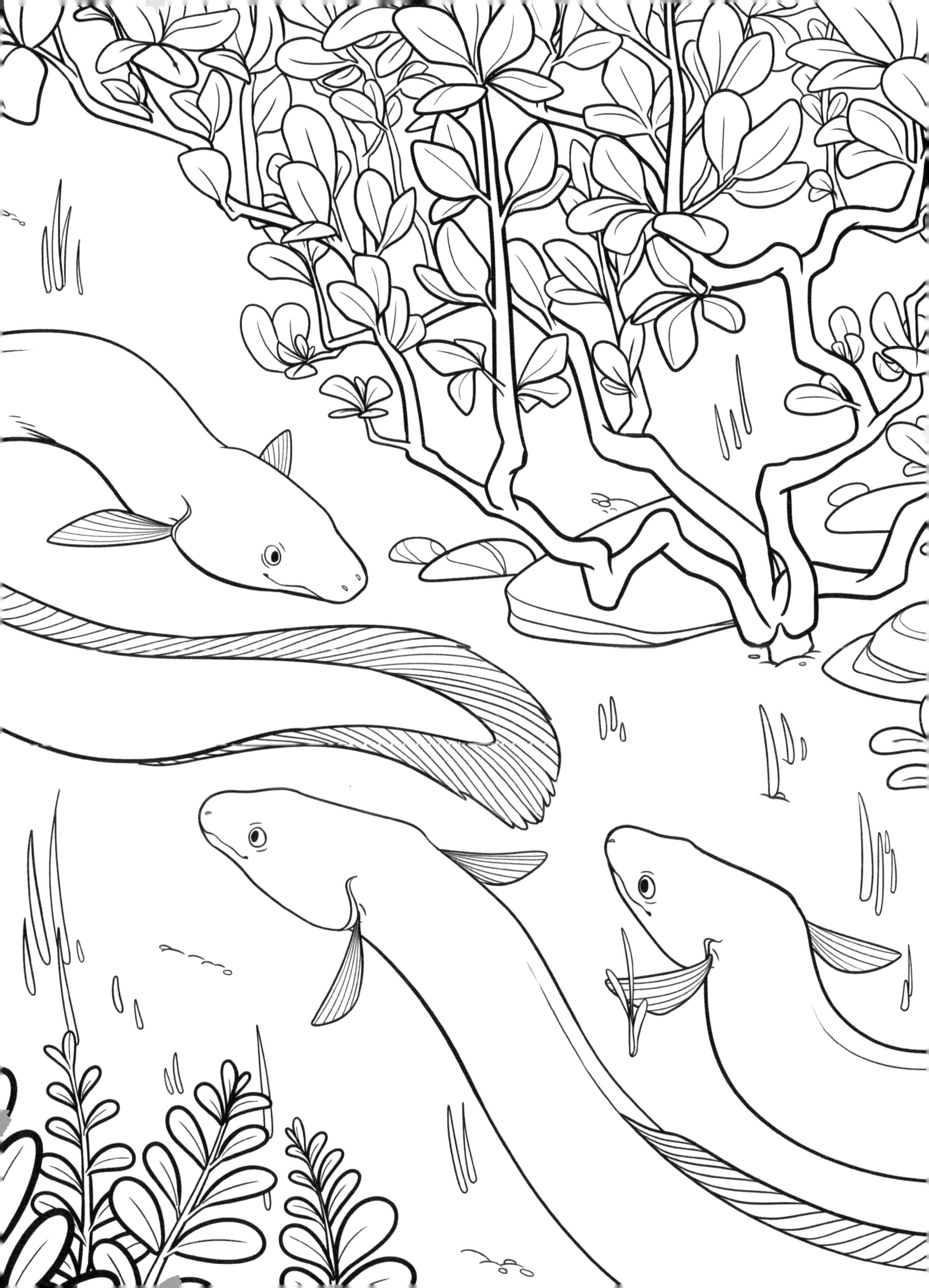

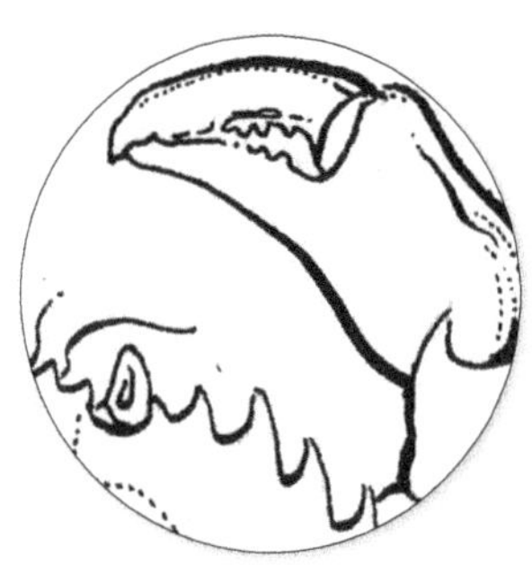

Invasive species

Zach Schrange, illustrator

Sailing ships bound for the Cape Cod region from Europe during the mid-1800s unknowingly carried aboard an unwelcome passenger. The ballast water was a perfect place for European green crabs to stow away. When ballasts were dumped into the bay, the crab quickly adapted to the new surroundings. Today, the European green crab is abundant along the East Coast, ranging from Delaware to Nova Scotia. It thrives in the colder shallow estuary water of salt marshes, sandy beaches, and rocky coasts. This voracious predictor is capable of crushing and feasting on more than 35 soft-shelled clams, scallops, mussels, and other mollusks every day. Particularly aggressive, the green crab out-competes native mud crabs, shellfish, and other animals that depend on the same food and habitat to survive. Thirty years ago, the European green crab was discovered on the Pacific Coast, and is now wreaking havoc in the ecosystems of San Francisco Bay and British Columbia.

Invasive species, such as the European green crab, can negatively impact native species diversity and disrupt an ecosystem's balance.

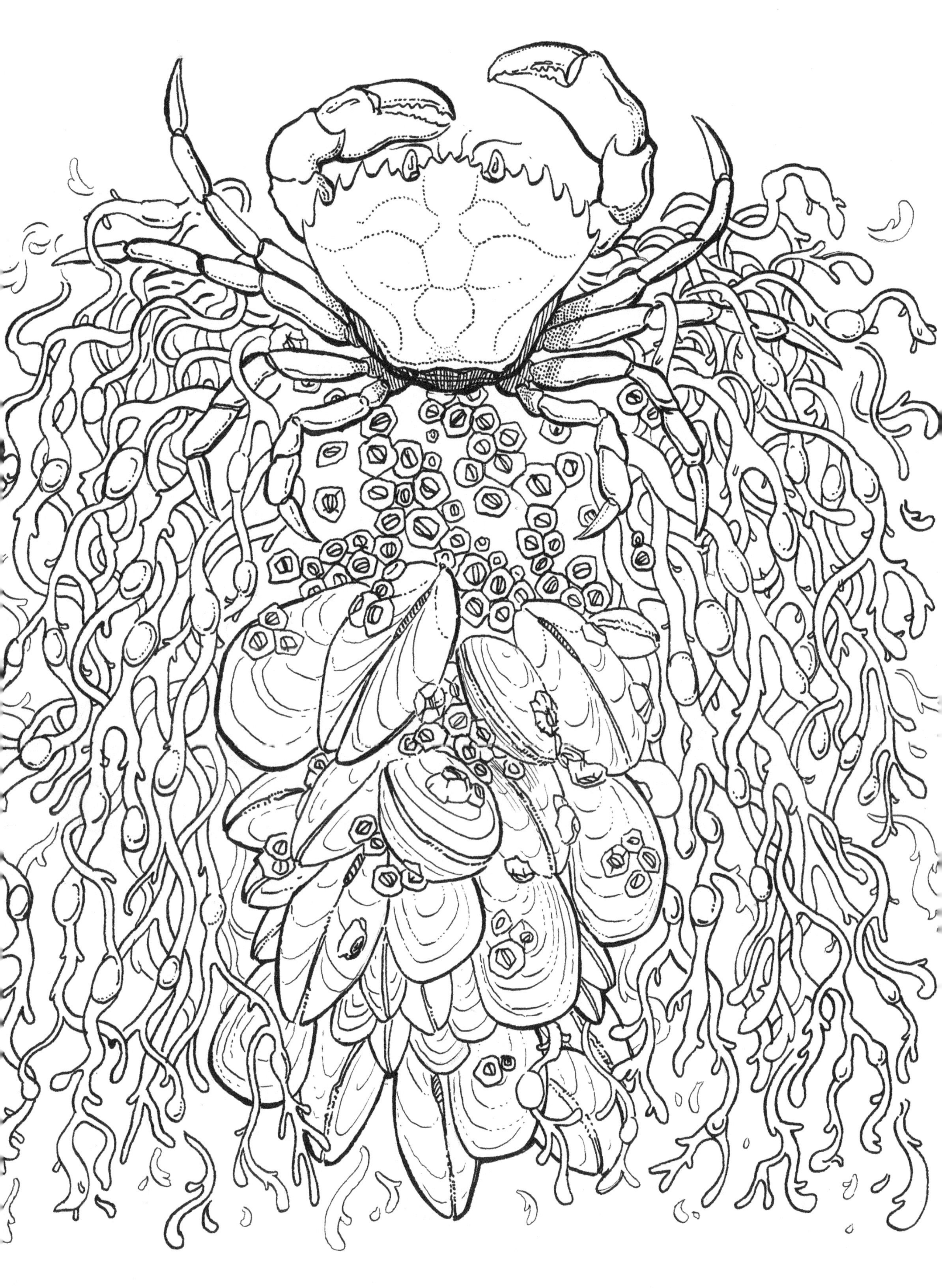

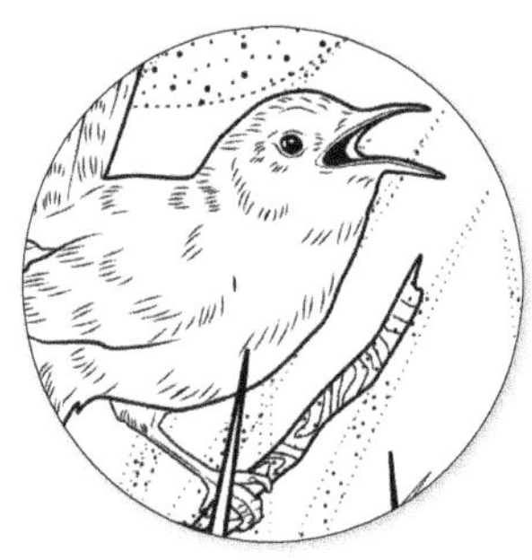

Music of the marsh

Kara Perilli, illustrator

The noises in the salt marsh can be musical. Wind-rustling marsh reeds harmonizing with the insect cacophony is set to the rhythm of the moving tide. Rusty-brown marsh wrens engage in complex call-and-answer duets, singing a repertoire of over 100 variations that lasts all hours of the day and into the night. Accompanying the ensemble is the raucous voice of a hidden clapper rail, adding loud series of chock-chock-chock-chock-chock that rapidly decrescendos into silence. An array of acoustical components blend together, creating a symphony in the marsh.

Marsh wrens will fiercely defend their territory, often building ten or more "dummy nests" to assure another wren won't nest nearby. Clapper rails are very secretive, staying hidden between the dense stalks of marsh grasses. Occasionally, rails will forage for food along the edges of an exposed mud flat.

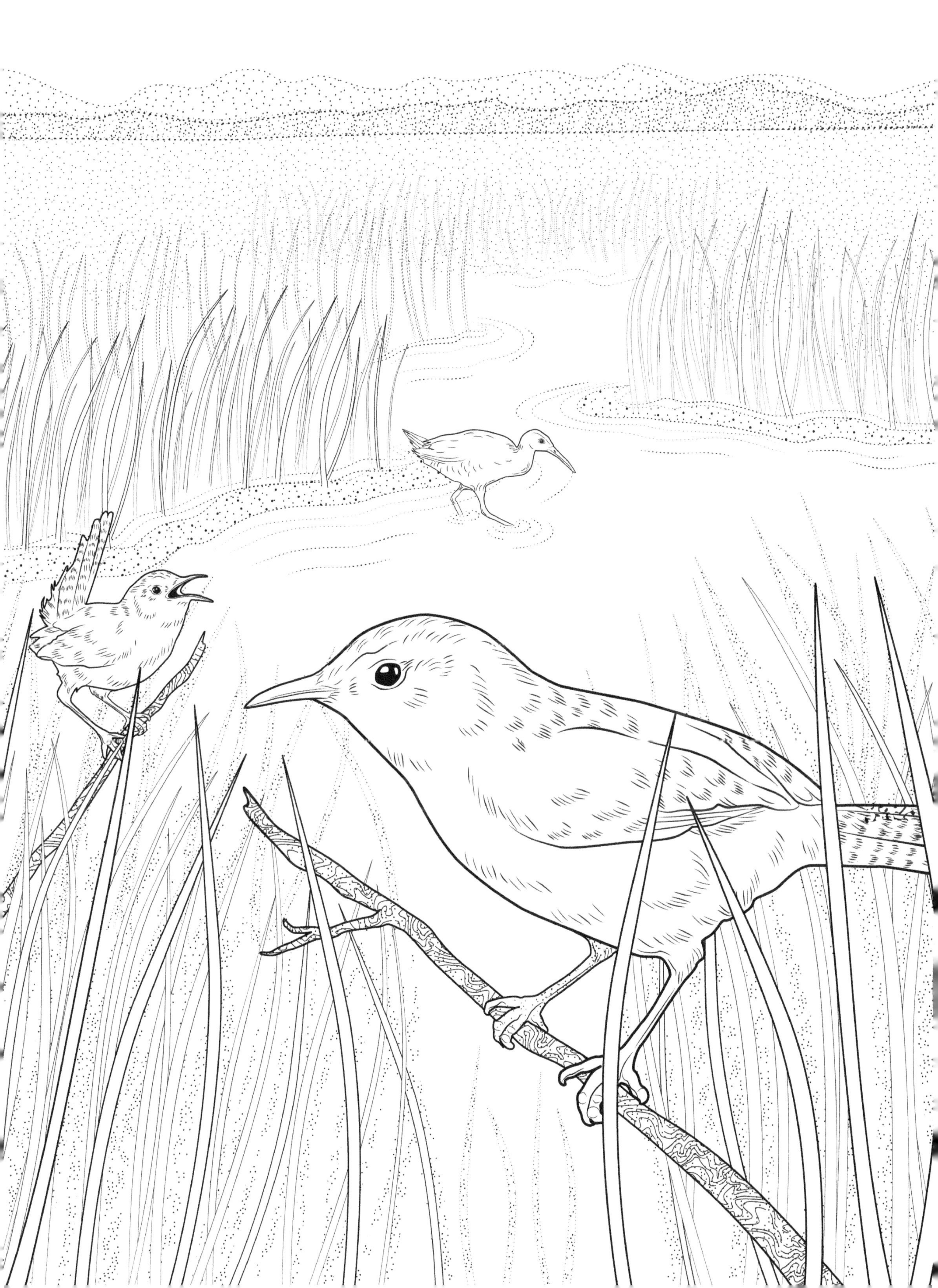

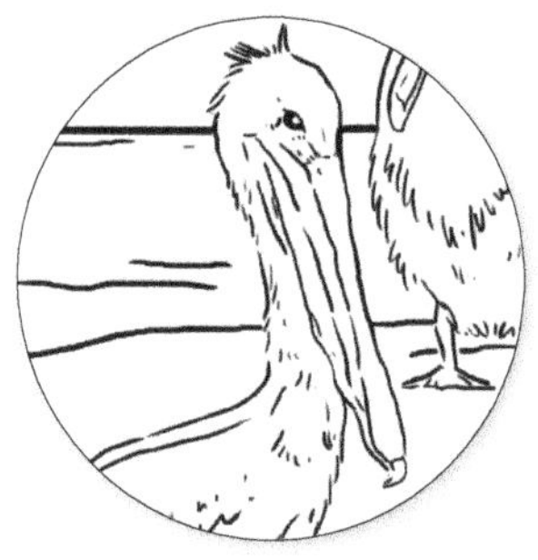

Nesting island

Amy Yeager, illustrator

Brown pelicans nest in secluded locations, like isolated islands. Several hundred birds will nest together in a colony. Finding the right spot is important since nests can be on the ground, in shrubs or mangroves, or even ten feet above the water in trees. For about 30 days the parent birds take turns protecting the nest by gently standing on the eggs. Pinkish hatchlings emerge without any down or feathers, and are blind. The vulnerable chicks are closely brooded by their parents, and will soon sport a coat of fuzzy white down, demanding to be fed. By the time the young birds are five to six weeks old, they will venture out of the nest and toddle clumsily on the ground. The toddlers socialize in a crèche during the day, but the parents are somehow able to find their own chicks to feed. By eight to ten weeks of age, the youngsters are ready to fledge, but still rely on parental guidance to learn fish diving techniques. The young birds stay close to their parents for about a year and will become parents themselves in three or four years.

Before the United States banned DDT and other pesticides in 1972, brown pelicans were extinct along the Louisiana coast and breeding colonies were severely decreased elsewhere. Within ten years the population of brown pelicans rebounded. Brown pelicans are once again common along much of the Gulf and Atlantic coasts. They have become regular summer visitors as far north as the New York and Jersey shore.

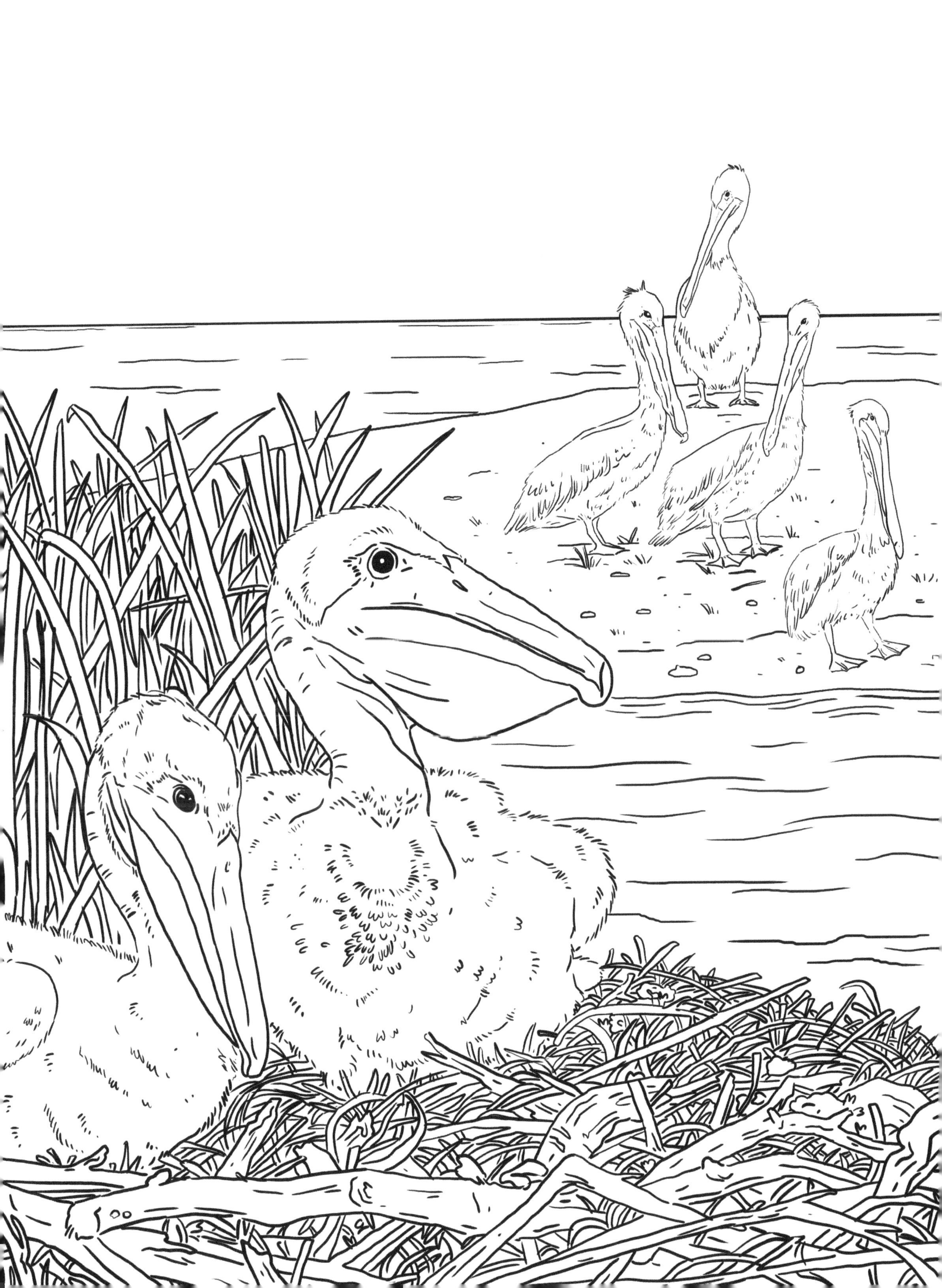

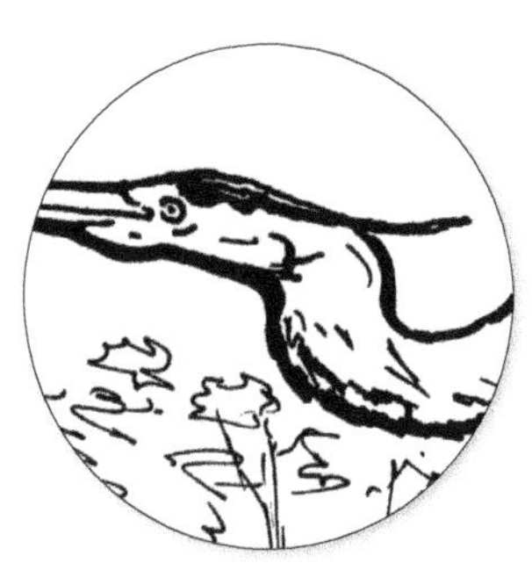

Icon of the wetlands

Cindy Billingsley, illustrator

Standing still at the water's edge, great blue heron are iconic of wetlands. Great blue herons are commonly found in salt marshes and freshwater bogs, along river banks and streams, and near lakes and ponds. These stately birds with elegant feathers traipse delicately through shallow water. They stalk patiently, sometimes freezing mid-stride, then with lightning quick reflexes, the long neck darts the dagger-like bill into the water to seize a meal. Fish, reptiles, rodents, amphibians, small birds, just about anything that moves in the water are fair game for the great blue. When startled, the heron takes flight with strong graceful wing beats while issuing a guttural "gwonk" farewell.

Herons, egrets, and terns were once mercilessly slaughtered by the hundreds of thousands, often for just a few highly prized feathers to adorn ladies hats. The snowy egret was on the verge of extinction by 1896, when outrage finally triggered a women-lead boycott of the feather trade. The Massachusetts Audubon Society was organized to expose this senseless massacre of birds just for fashion's sake. Other states followed suit with chapters to support the boycott, and in 1905, The National Association of Audubon Societies was formed. Thirty-five years later, the organization became the National Audubon Society.

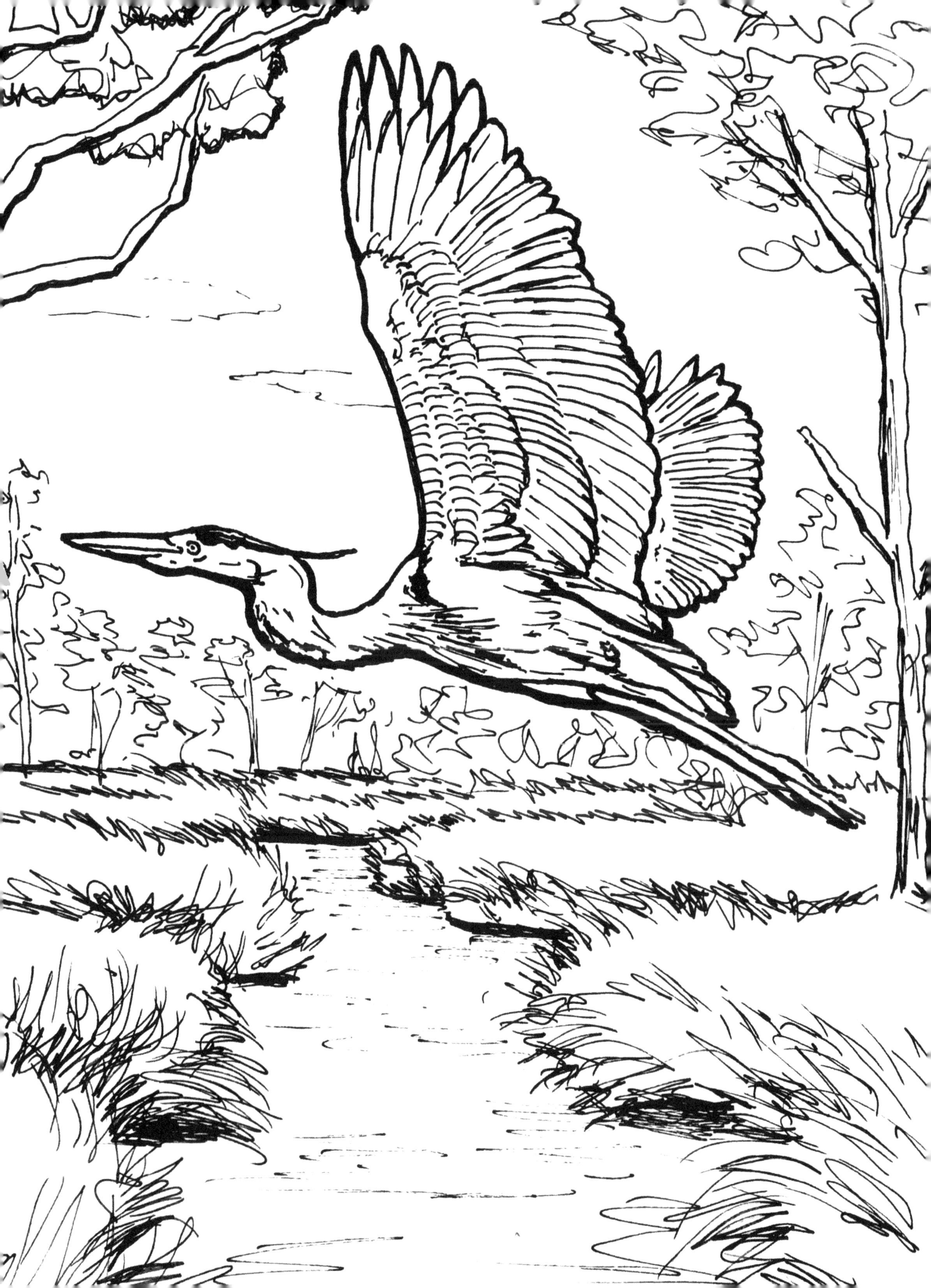

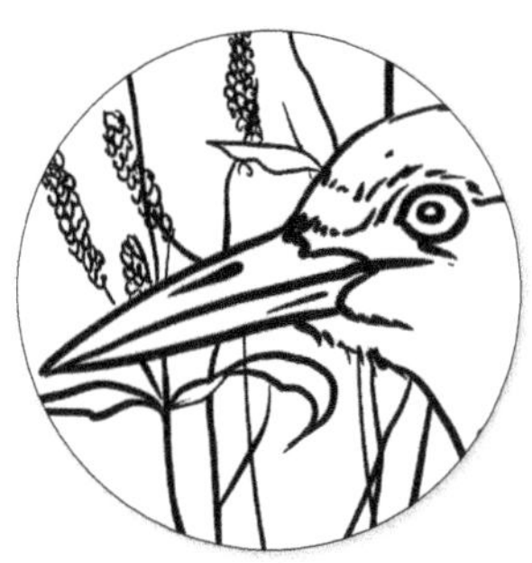

Night stalker

Carrie Carlson, illustrator

Under the cover of darkness, a small hunchbacked heron stalks along the edge of the marsh. Cloaked in a striking black cape with a long white plume trailing off the cap, the black-crowned night-heron looks the part of a sinister villain. This solitary figure silently forages for small fish, shrimp or crabs along the fringes of the mud flats. Though solitary in its hunting forays, the black-crowned night-heron is actually a social bird. Often nesting in colonies with other herons, ibises, even pelicans, a dozen or more black-crowned night-heron nests may be in one tree. Adult birds do not recognize their own young and will take care of birds from other nests. Young birds stay together on the ground or cluster in the treetops. In the winter, black-crowned night-herons roost together during the day.

Black-crowned night-herons have a reputation of causing havoc in tern colonies, snatching young birds in the middle of the night.

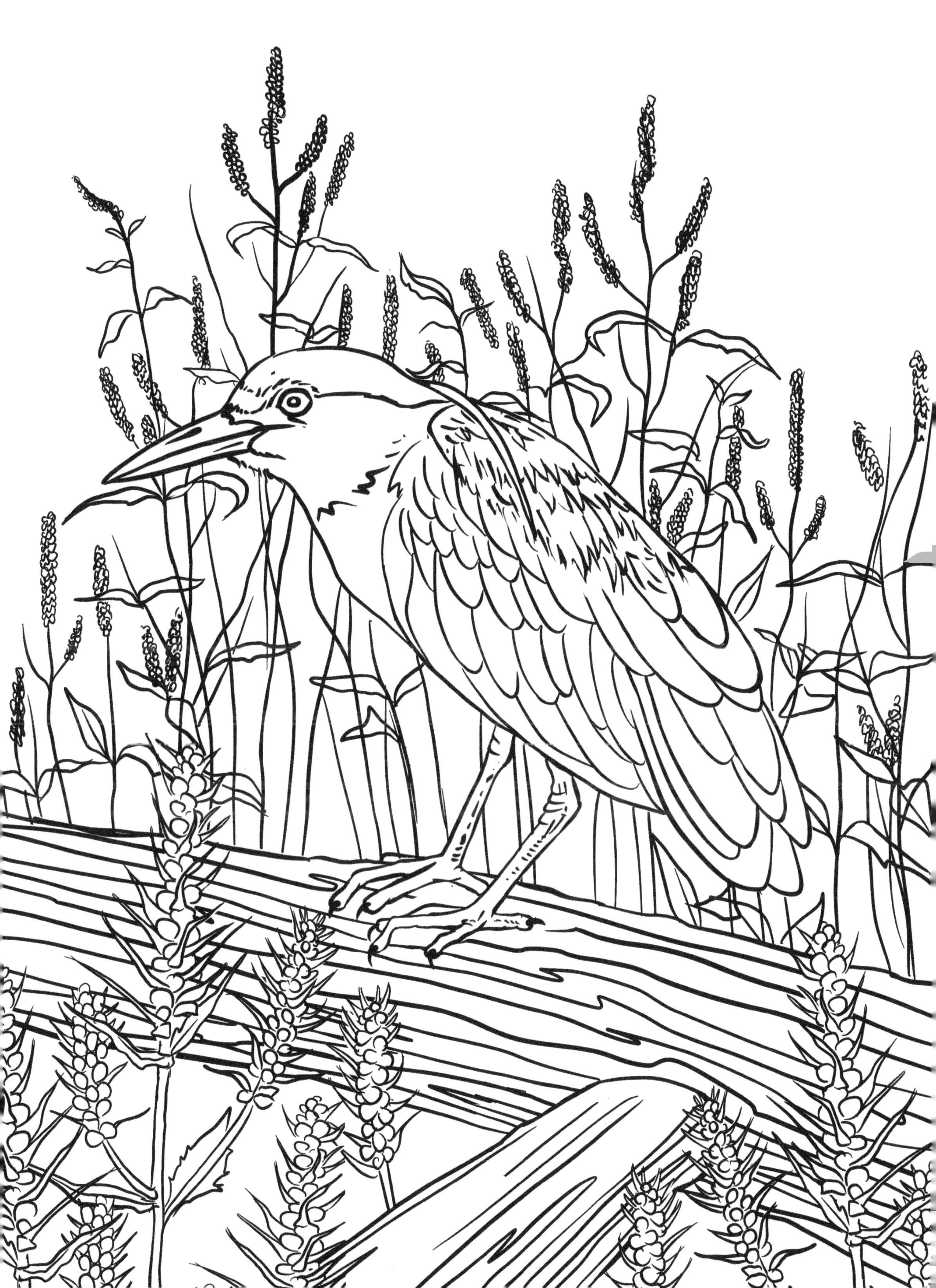

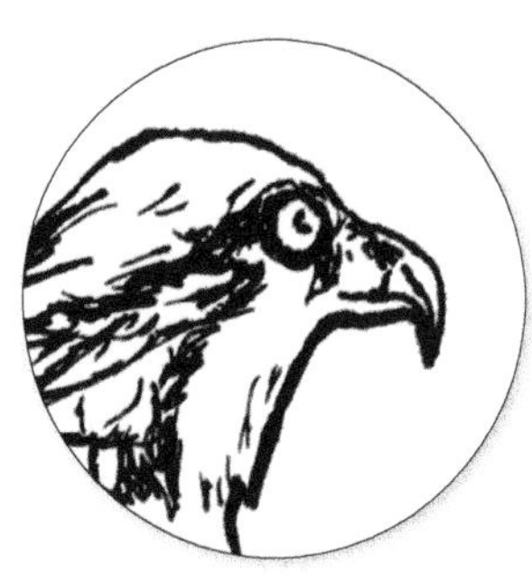

Fishing from the sky

Cindy Billingsley, illustrator

Ospreys can be found just about anywhere there is a large expanse of water with fish. Though common throughout coastal estuaries, ospreys are also familiar farther inland around large lakes and rivers, even water reservoirs. The white head of the osprey with a broad brown eye stripe makes this large raptor easy to recognize. In flight, the distinctive kink in the osprey's outstretched wings, looks like the letter "M" soaring high in the sky. Flying at heights of 50 feet, the osprey uses exceptionally keen eyesight to detect a fish in the water below. After a slight hover, the osprey will plunge head first in a rapid dive. At the last second, it will pull up and extend its legs, going talons first into the water. Often the osprey will completely submerge as it snags the fish. Immediately on surfacing, the bird takes to the air, shaking briefly like a wet dog. If successful in fishing, the osprey will carefully turn the fish head-first-into-the-wind for more aerodynamic control while flying to a tree or platform to enjoy its meal.

Ospreys select nesting sites that are often above or very near water: channel markers, trees, man-made platforms erected in the estuaries or lakeside, or even cell phone and radio towers. An osprey pair form a lifelong bond. They will return to the same nest every year, adding new nesting material each season.

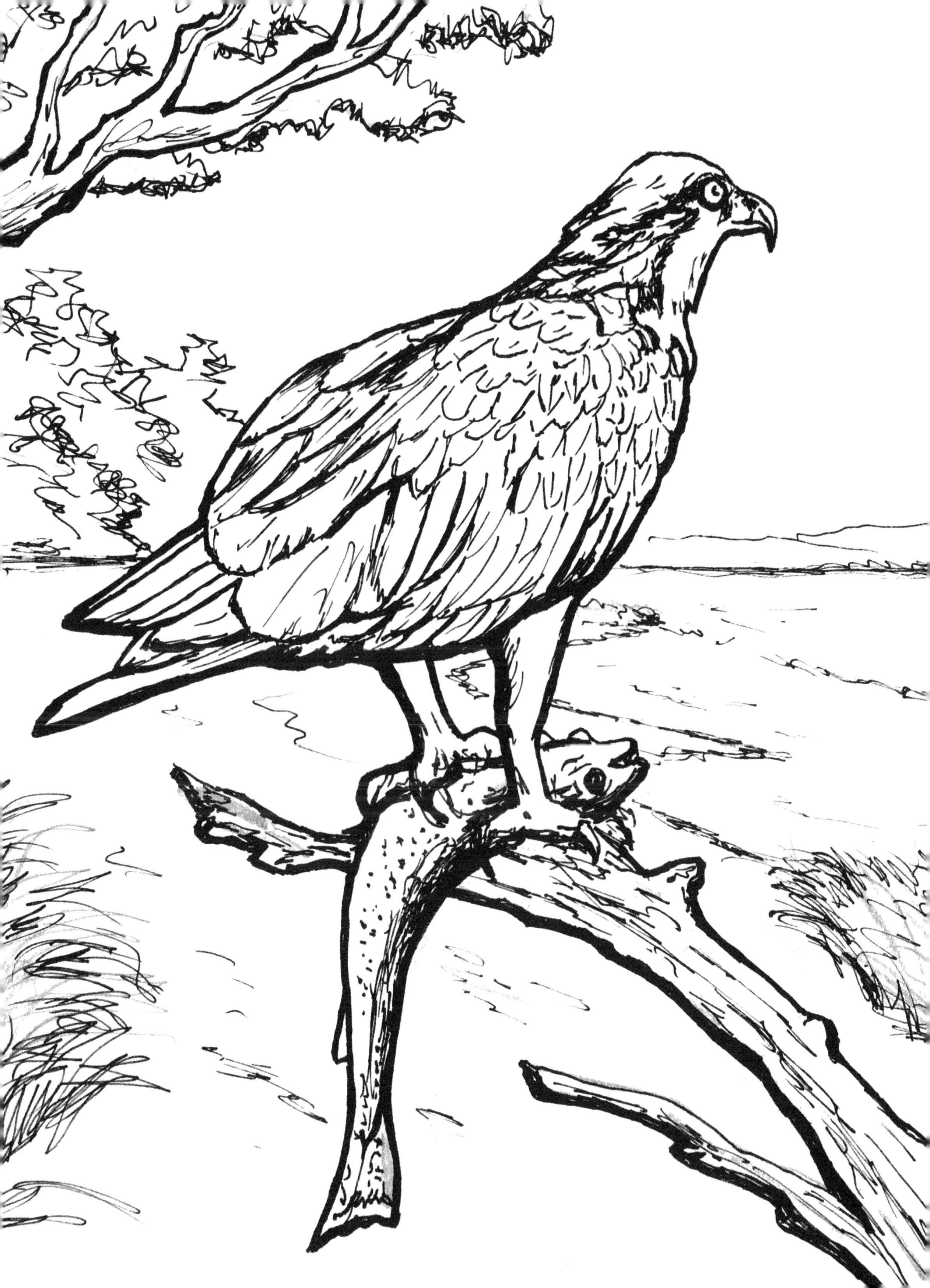

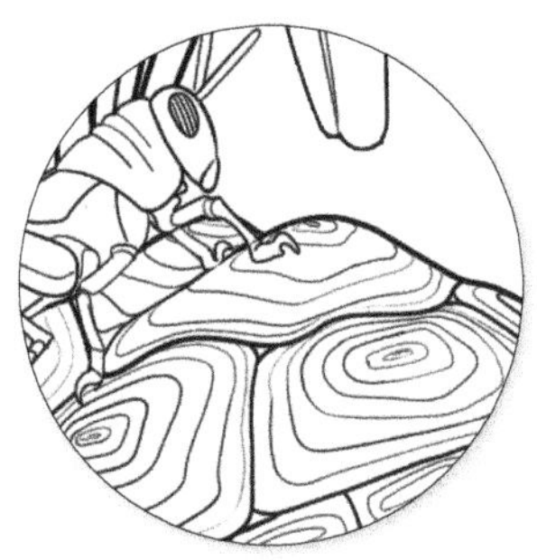

Diamond in the marsh

Sami Hernandez, illustrator

The diamondback terrapin is the only reptile adapted to live exclusively in the estuary. The scutes on its carapace are adorned with beautiful concentric diamond patterns and grooves. This turtle species spends almost its whole life in brackish water, but still needs freshwater to survive. Rain collects as a layer on top of the brackish water, and the terrapin will come to the surface for a sip. The female terrapin ventures onto land seeking high ground to deposit about half a dozen or more eggs in shallow gourd-shaped nest. Her search to find a safe nesting spot may take her across busy roads or highways. This path may prove fatal, as cars speed by with no regard to her plight. Terrapins can live 25 years, but face significant threats to their survival because of human-related activities. Pollution, loss of habitat, lack of safe nesting locations, along with entrapment in crab pots and fishing gear are their biggest obstacles.

Diamondback terrapins were once so abundant in the estuaries, fisherman considered them a nuisance. That was before the terrapins became a target species worth $90 or more for a dozen. Demand for terrapin meat was high in the 1920s. Terrapins were hunted to near-extinction to sate the appetite high society had for turtle soup. Terrapins are no longer used in soups, but their population has not recovered sufficiently over the past years. Harvesting diamondback terrapins is now banned in every state along the Atlantic coast.

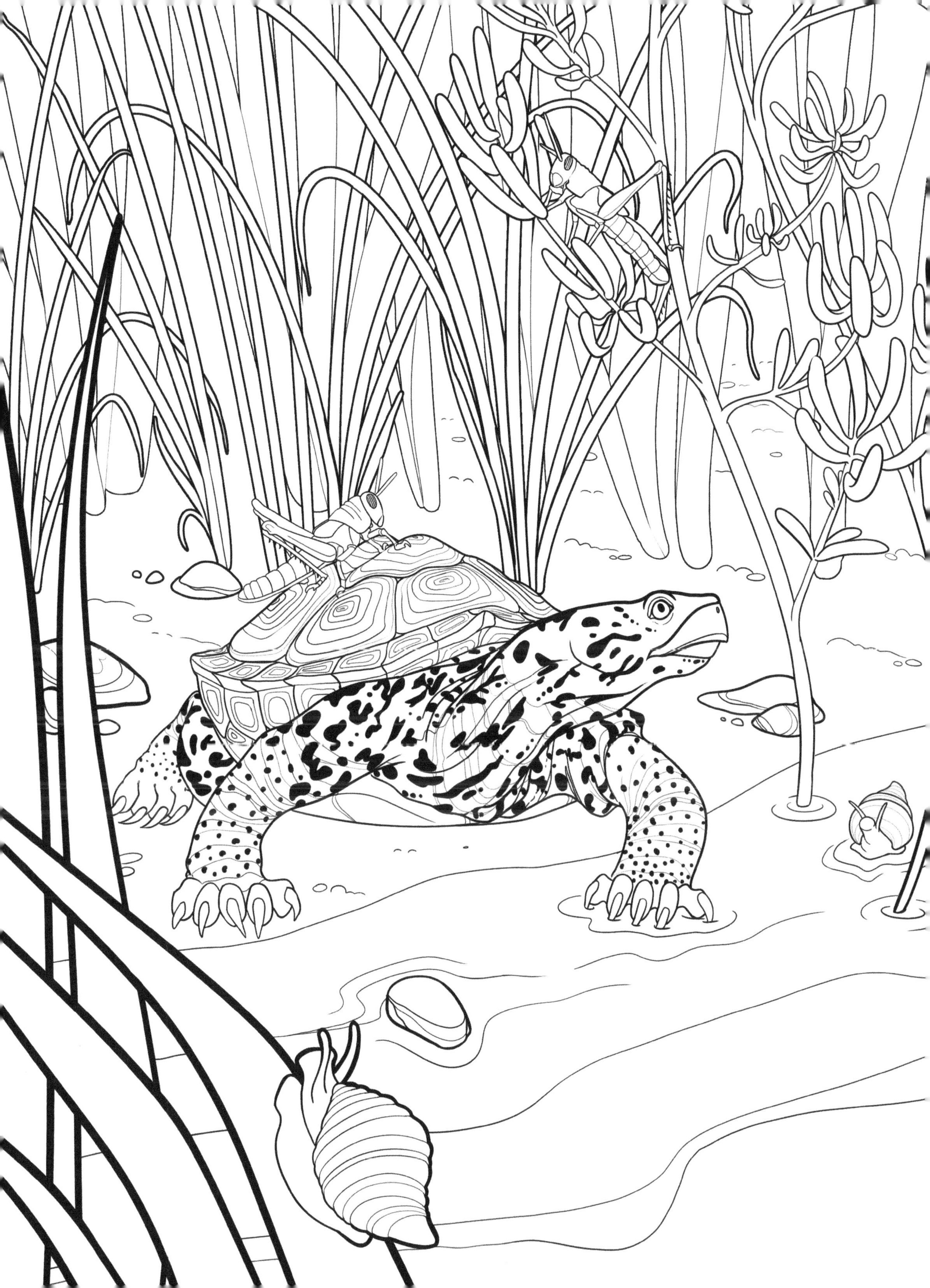

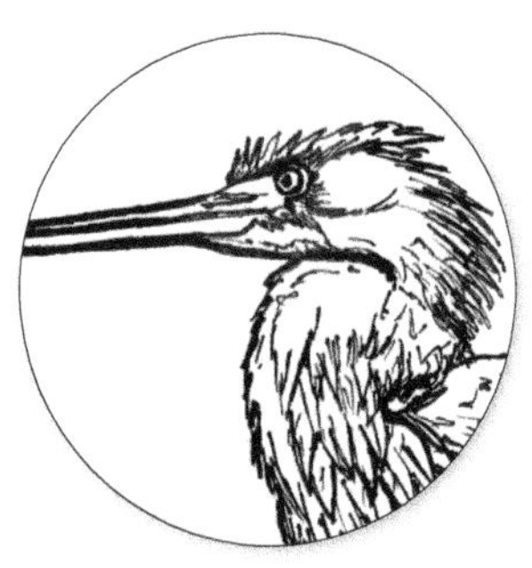

Beautiful dancer

Cindy Billingsley, illustrator

The tricolored heron is a beautiful bird. Called a Louisiana heron in the past, it is a delicate-looking, colorful heron, mostly blue-gray with splotches of purple and white on its body. Distinctive white stripes of feathers run down the length of the long slender neck. The juvenile tricolored heron has reddish disheveled feathers on its head and neck, but the white feathers are present down its neck. The tricolored heron executes a graceful dance along the marsh edge. Short runs, sudden pauses, quick turns and gentle slides are performed before jabbing its bill quickly to seize a fish, crab, or other morsel from the shallow water.

The oldest recorded tricolored heron was at least 17 years, 8 months old when it was shot in the Bahamas in 1976. The band on the bird's leg was from Virginia in 1958.

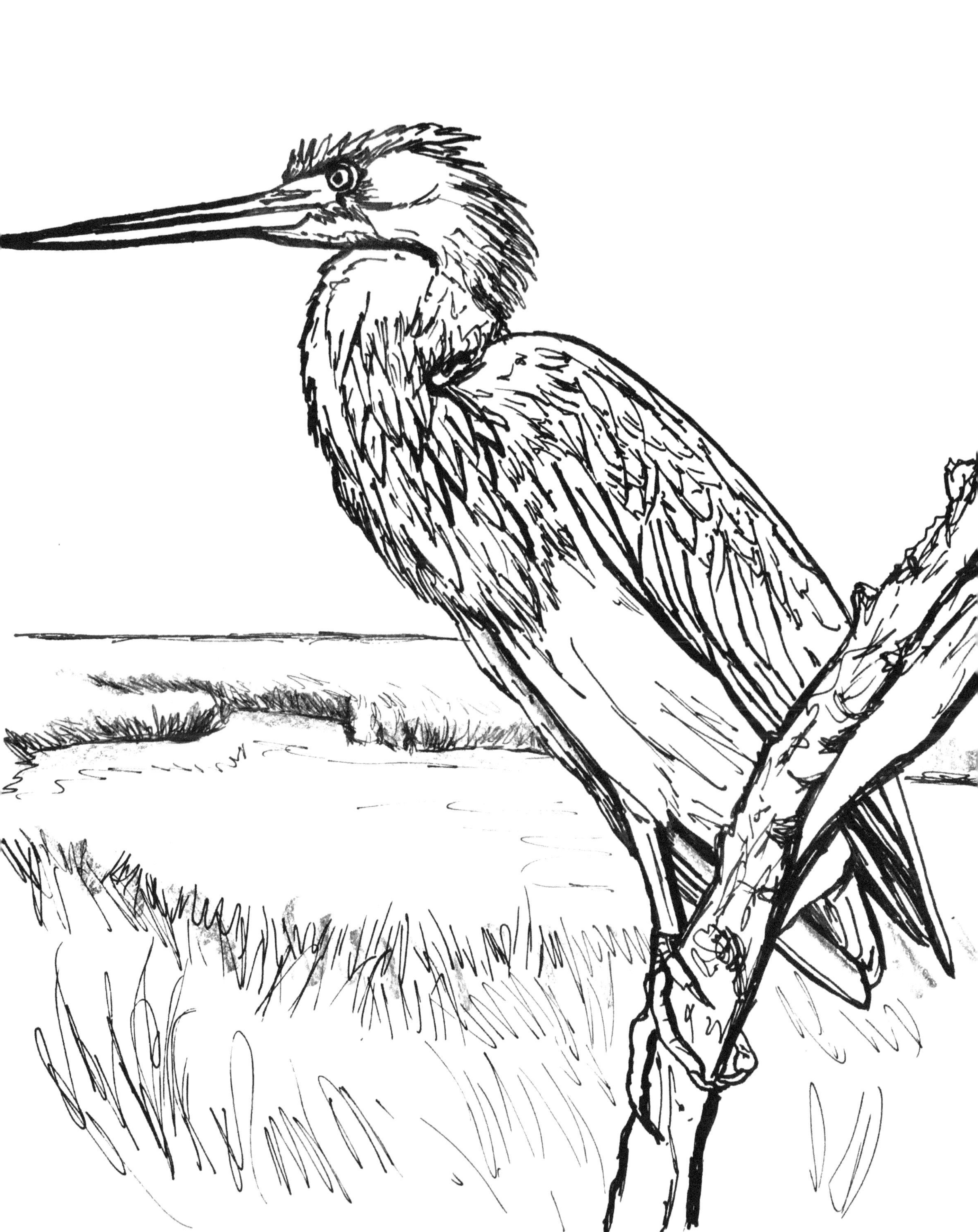

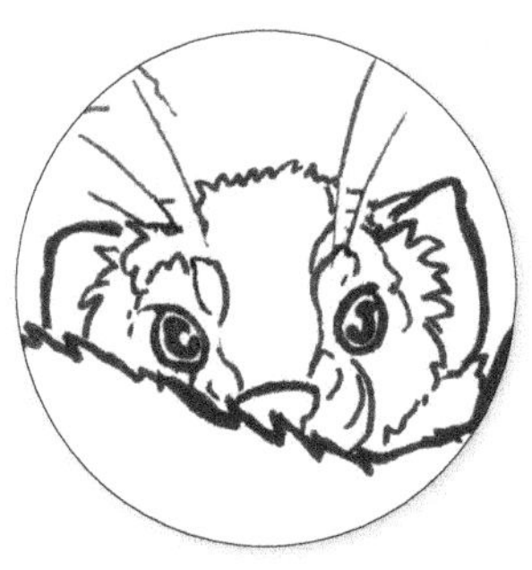

Tidal creek

Tiffany Miller Russell, illustrator

Upland creeks drain freshwater into the brackish estuary. Along these creeks, the American mink stakes out its territory. Easily mistaken from a distance for river otters, minks have a smaller and more slender stature. They are solitary individuals, except for mating season. These opportunistic feeders are particularly fond of swimming underwater, hunting for fish and crawdads. Minks do not hesitate to snag a fish that is much larger than themselves. They have a tendency to kill more than the amount of food needed, and can cause serious damage to bird and native animal populations. Fur farm escapes have contributed to American minks extending their range into new areas.

American minks have webbed feet and can swim up to 100 feet underwater. Their highly prized soft fur is covered with oil to repel water.

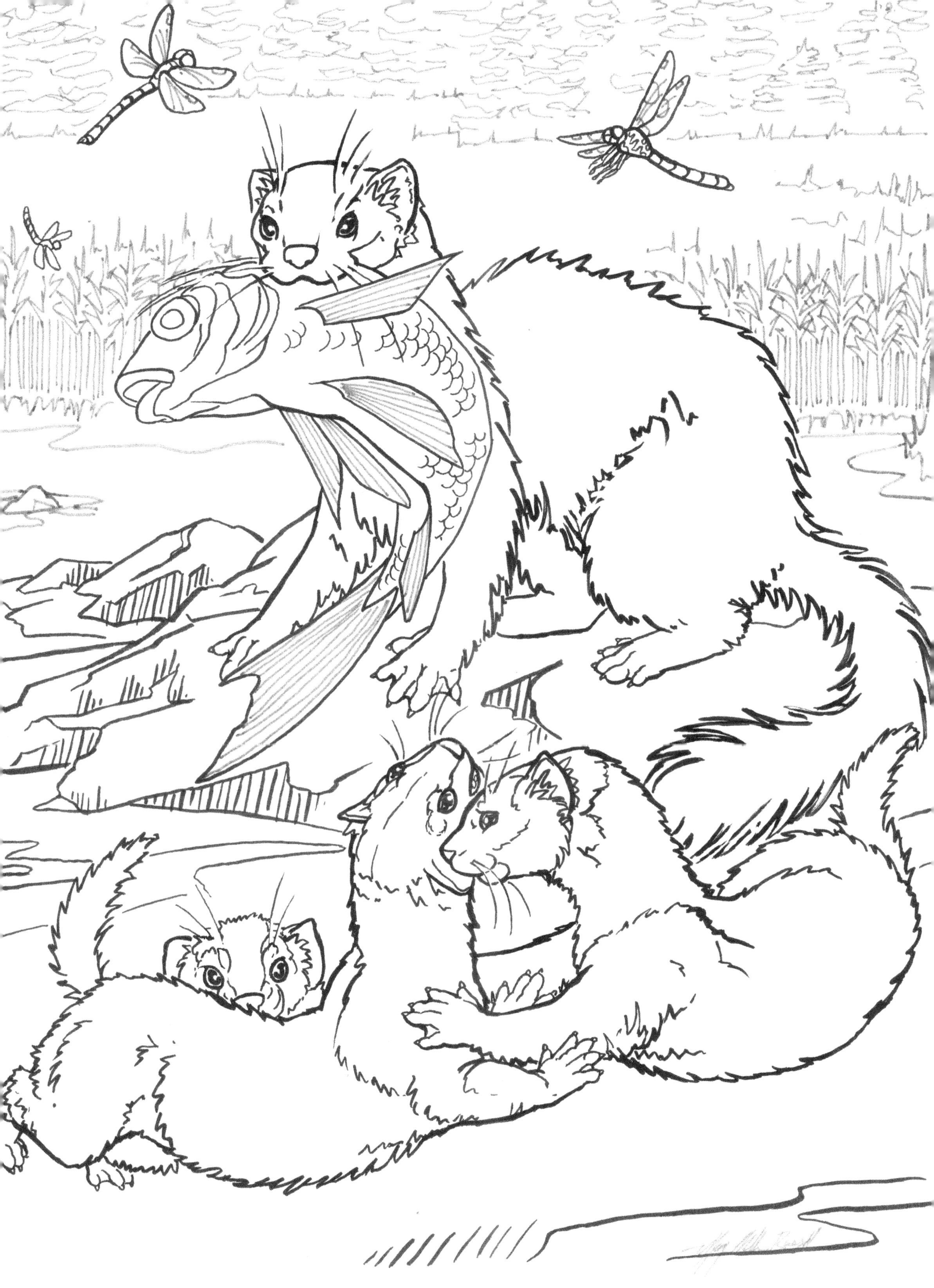

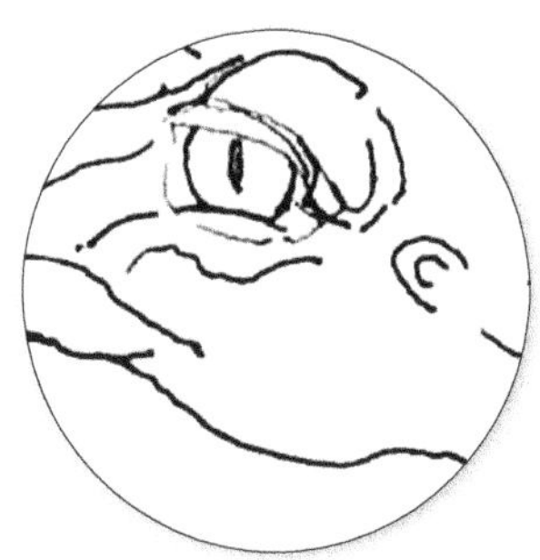

Coastal floodplain

Susan Fox, illustrator

Riparian zones are found along the river banks where trees and water-loving animals thrive. Low, flat land that spreads out from the river channel is the floodplain. Periodic flooding during heavy rains allows the floodplain to stay soggy for long periods of time, creating a rich wetland habitat for fish, amphibians, reptiles, and birds. The American alligator is a prominent resident in the floodplains. Living exclusively in freshwater, alligators will occasionally venture into the estuaries, though they cannot tolerate even slight levels of salinity for extended periods of time. Ibises, egrets, and herons also take advantage of the rich food supply in the floodplain wetland habitats.

Alligators have been living on Earth for nearly 200 million years. They somehow avoided extinction 65 million years ago when the dinosaurs died off, only to be faced with that possibility again in the 1950s. Demand for alligator skin and uncontrolled hunting almost wiped out the species. In 1967, the alligator gained federal protection under the Endangered Species Act. Within twenty years, populations rebounded to the point where protection was no longer necessary. With over two million alligators in the southeastern United States now, managed hunting programs are in place to keep the population in check.

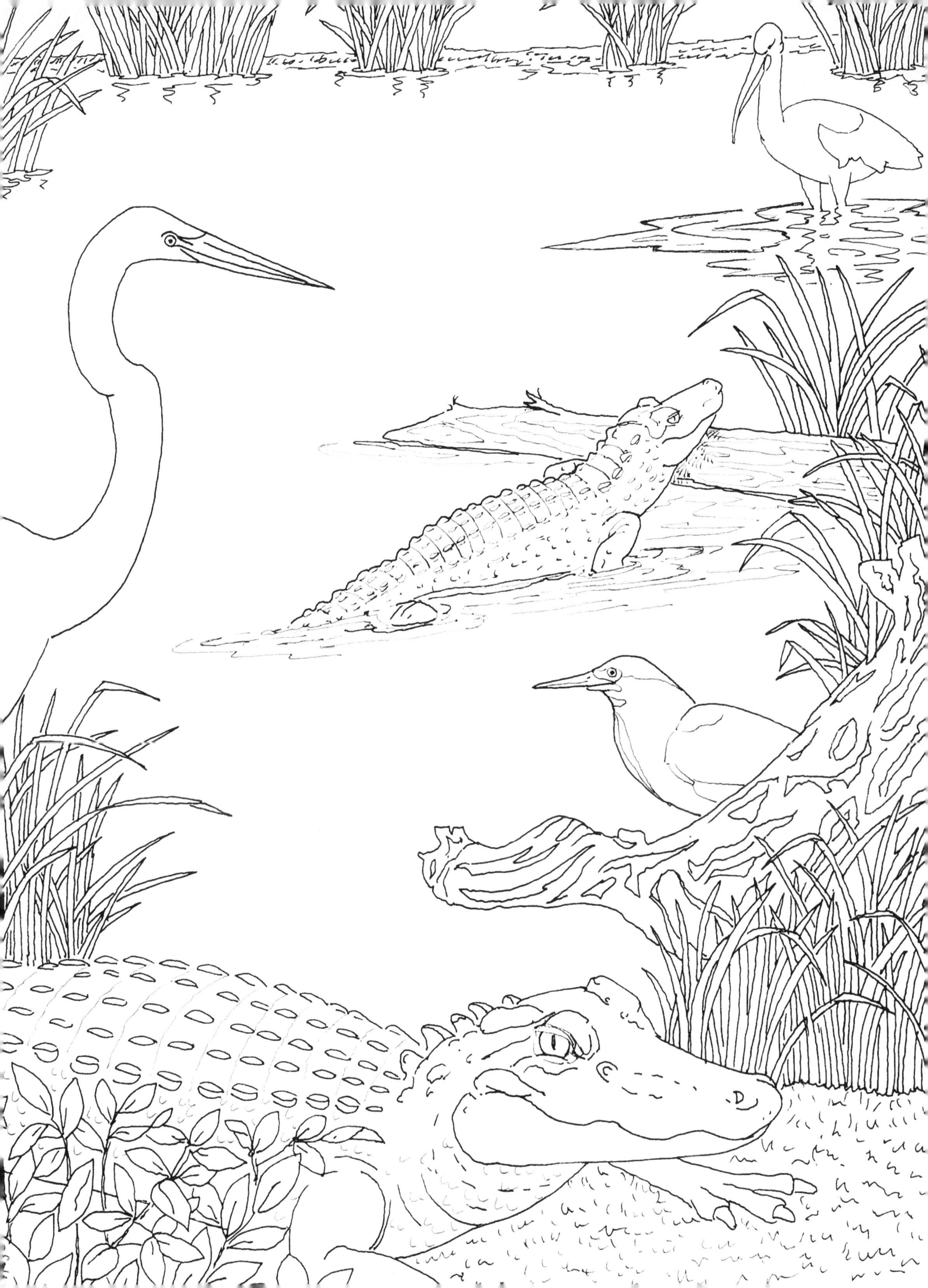

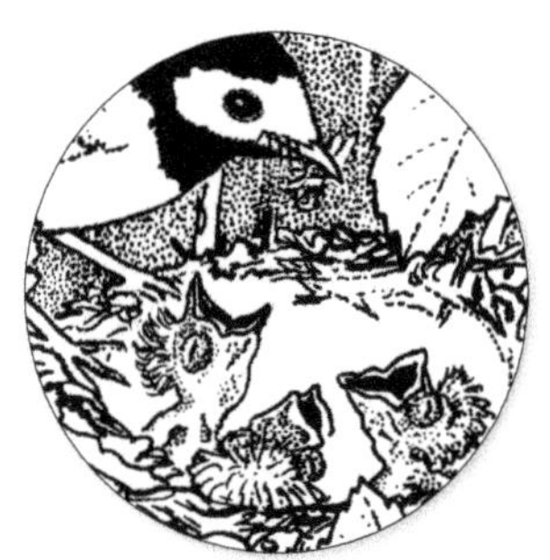

Deep in the cypress swamp

Anne Runyon, illustrator

Sunlight barely penetrates the thick canopy of vegetation that engulfs the swamp with an eerie atmosphere. Forested wetlands dominated by cypress and tupelo trees set apart a swamp from a grass-covered marsh. Natural freshwater saturates the soil, making it water-logged muck. Water, littered with organic decay, seems to stand still as it flows ever-so-slowly through the swamp. Low country cypress swamps permeate the southeastern coastal plains. Flocks of warblers and other songbirds often roam the forest canopy, while reptiles, amphibians, and a myriad of insects find homes in the murkiness below. Small mammals seek hide-aways among the dense vegetation, hoping to elude detection by predators. Spooky sounds add to the mysterious aura deep in the cypress swamp.

Many secrets are hidden in the swamp forest. Can you find the following?

Red-bellied water snake
Brimley's chorus frog
Spinybacked orb weaver spider
Marsh rabbit
Hooded warblers and their nest of young
Bald cypress trees
Tupelo gum tree
Swamp rose

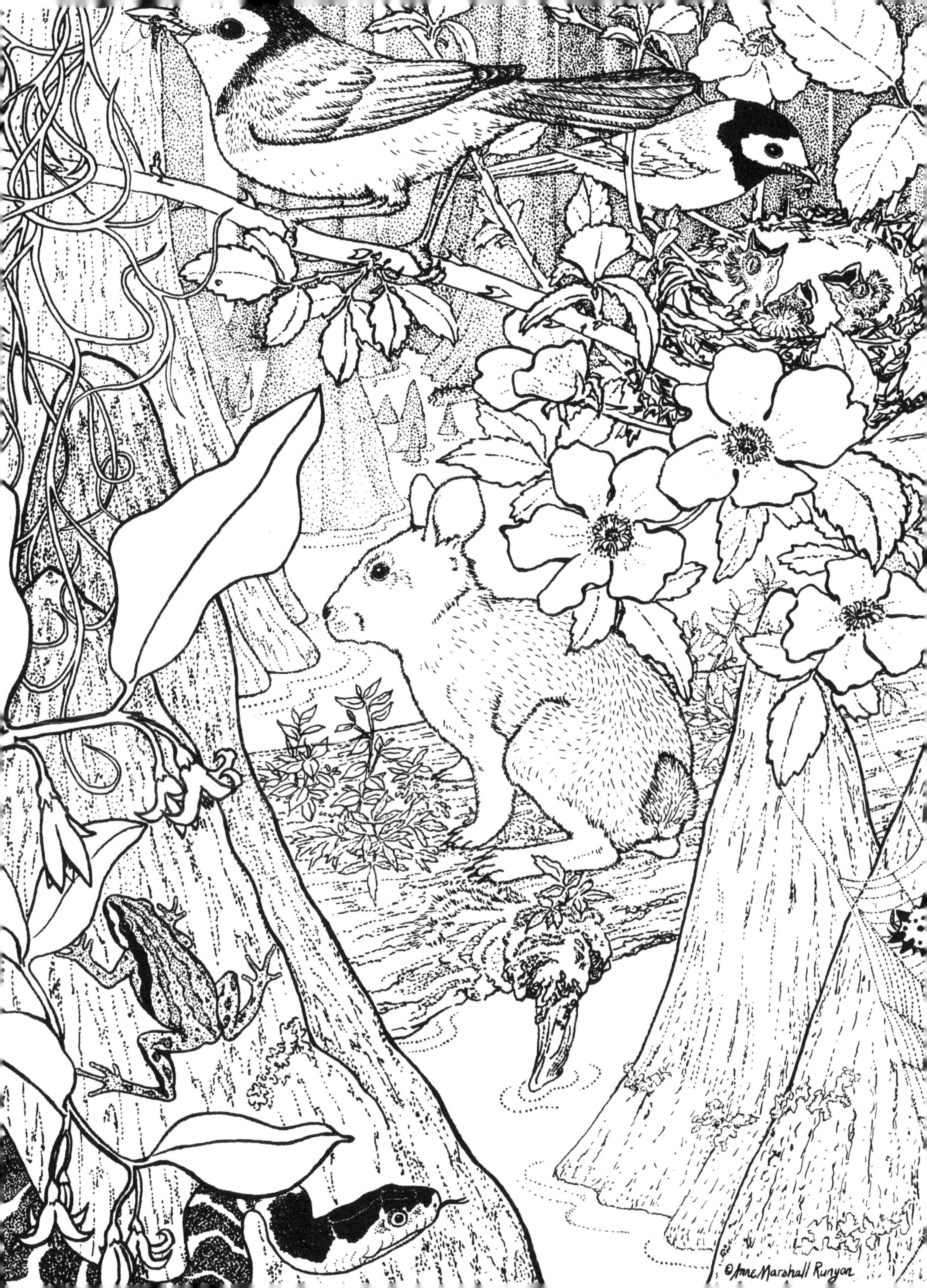
©Anne Marshall Runyon

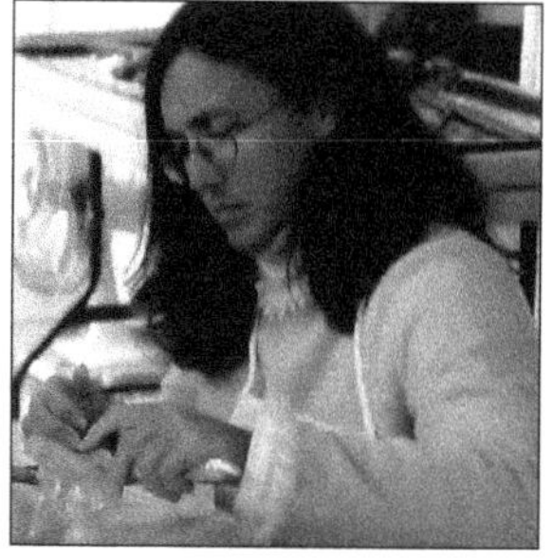

CINDY BILLINGSLEY, *Great blue heron (introduction) Icon of the wetlands, Beautiful dancer, Fishing from the sky*

Cindy is a professional studio artist based in TN. Cindy studied Fine Art and Illustration at Harris School of Art. She is an accomplished, self-taught wildlife and figurative sculptor. Cindy creates public art projects, paintings, and portraits, and sculpts in bronze and clay for exhibitions, galleries, and commissions. She also creates production art for companies. She exhibits nationally and internationally. Her art has evolved around social issues in the past few years, including the plight of endangered wildlife and the effects of Alzheimer's disease.

ELIZABETH BONERT, *Feeding frenzy, On the verge of extinction, Inshore secrets*

elizabethbonert.com | @elizabethbonert

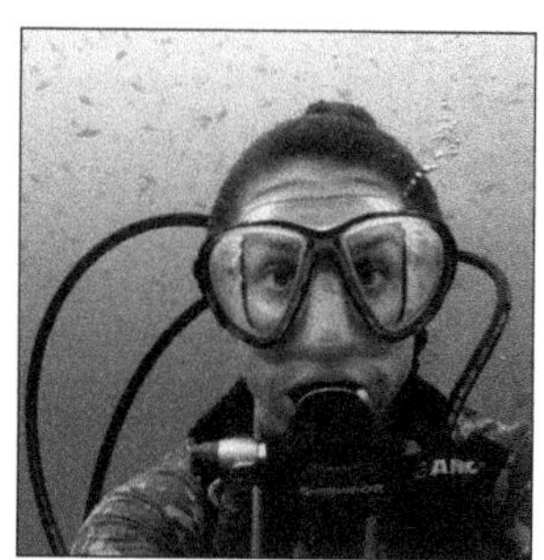

Elizabeth Bonert is a graphic designer and illustrator based in St. Petersburg, FL. She studied at the University of South Florida St. Petersburg, graduating with a BFA with a concentration in Graphic Design. Growing up exploring Florida, she has always loved to illustrate the marine life she has encountered. Over the years her subjects have expanded to other environments and species, inspired by her travels around the world. Passionate about the environment and combining the arts and sciences, she volunteers in the field and creates infographics for the Florida Fish and Wildlife Conservation Commission.

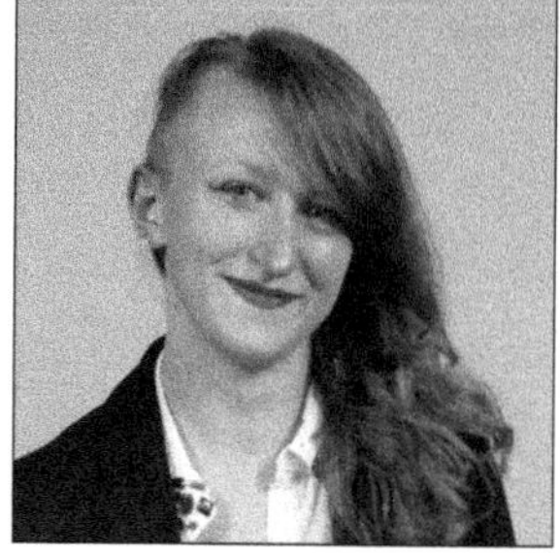

CASS GRAYBEAL BROWN, *Leviathans of the sea, Rocky seafloor*

grayillu.com

Cassandra Brown majored in Illustration at Savannah College of Art and Design. While in school, she focused on and minored in scientific illustration. Currently she is located in upstate NY with her husband and pit bull. The rich landscape and vibrant wildlife that surrounds them fuels the creativity behind her traditional scientific style.

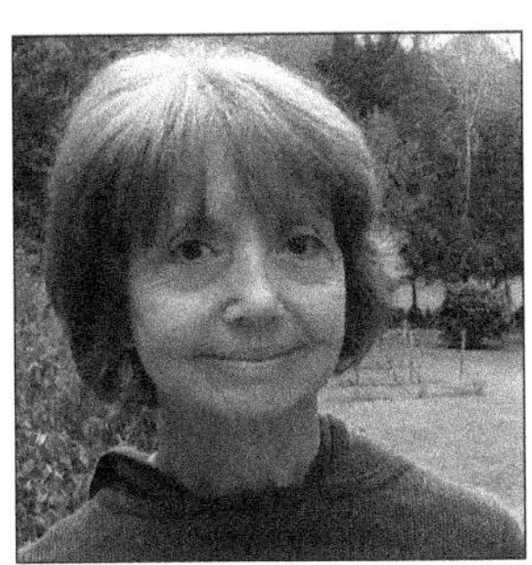

BONNIE CADOTTE, *At home in the sea*
piccolotales.com | blspino@yahoo.com

Bonnie Cadotte is a studio artist in Knoxville, TN, and works in a variety of mediums, letting the subject dictate the approach. She earned a BFA in Studio Art and a Master's in Education from the University of Tennessee, and has taught art in K-12 in private and public schools. Bonnie and her cousin, Lorraine Loria, started the publishing company, Piccolo Tales. Their first two children's books, *Wild About Manners* and *Wild About Friends*, are available on piccolotales.com. They are in the process of completing their third book.

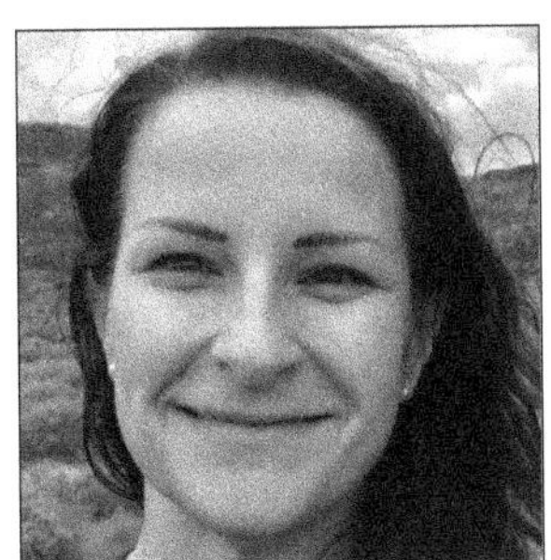

CARRIE CARLSON, *Between the dunes, Night stalker*
cscarlson.com | @bluebirdprintstudios

Carrie Carlson earned a BA in Biology and Art from Luther College, an MFA in Scientific Illustration from the University of Michigan, and an MA in Printmaking from Governors State University. Since 2001, she has been a full-time high school educator near Chicago. She has split her years between the science and art departments; teaching Drawing, Painting, International Baccalaureate Visual Arts, as well as Biology, Biomedical Sciences, and Horticulture. She also teaches a variety of adult art courses at the Morton Arboretum, including linoleum block printing, drawing birds, and field sketching.

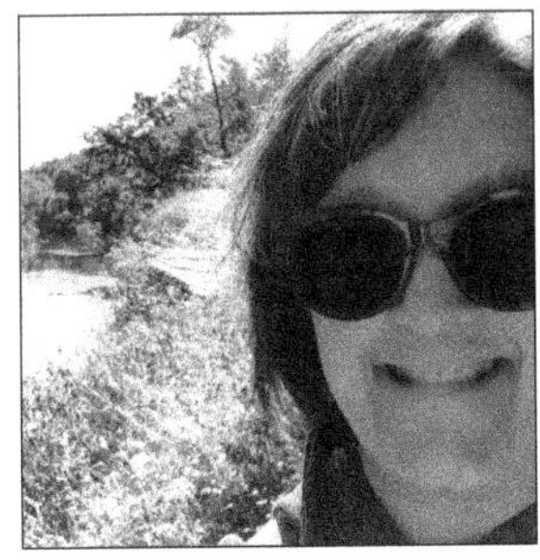

CAROL CREECH, *Live oak branch (title page illustration), Magnolia flower (for further reading page illustration)*
ccreechstudio.com

Carol Creech is a nature illustrator and maker based in Ann Arbor, MI. She enjoys creating with a variety of materials and her work includes traditional botanical and nature illustrations, natural stone jewelry and handmade journals. She holds a BA in Geography, an MILS in Library and Information Studies, and has taken courses at the Brookside Gardens School of Botanical Art and Illustration. She is a member of the Guild of Natural Science Illustrators (GNSI) and the American Society of Botanical Artists and has exhibited locally at Matthaei Botanical Gardens and regionally with other GNSI Great Lakes artists.

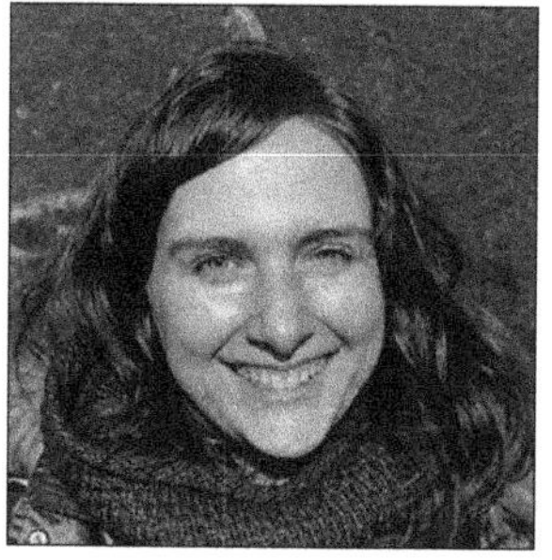

JENNIFER DEUTSCHER, *Wrack line*

alithographica.com

Jennifer (Jenn) Deutscher is a freelance scientific illustrator from Phoenix, AZ, currently based in NYC. She holds a BA in biological sciences and illustration from New York University, where she also worked for several years as a genetics research assistant, and received a certificate in botanical art and illustration from the New York Botanical Garden. Her work has appeared in galleries, museum exhibits, scientific journals, and educational materials internationally.

HEATHER DIVOKY, *Salt marsh engineers*

heatherdivoky.com

Heather Divoky is an artist living and working in Wilmington, NC. She has worked in the arts as a creator, curator, historian, designer, and administrator. Her primary concern is story-telling through great detail and color. Divoky works with marker, ink, wire, and stained glass, although she is always trying new media and techniques.

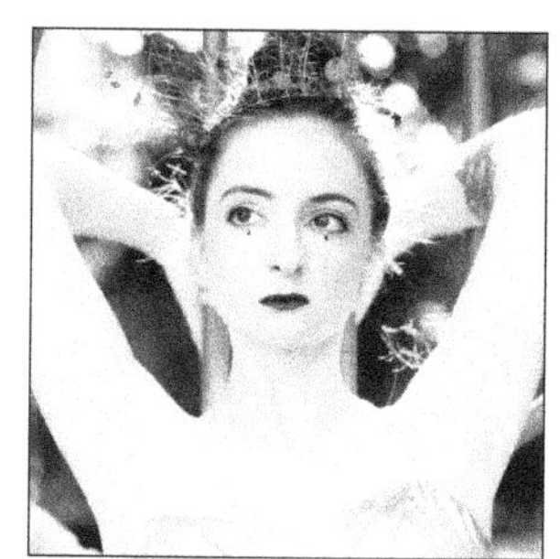

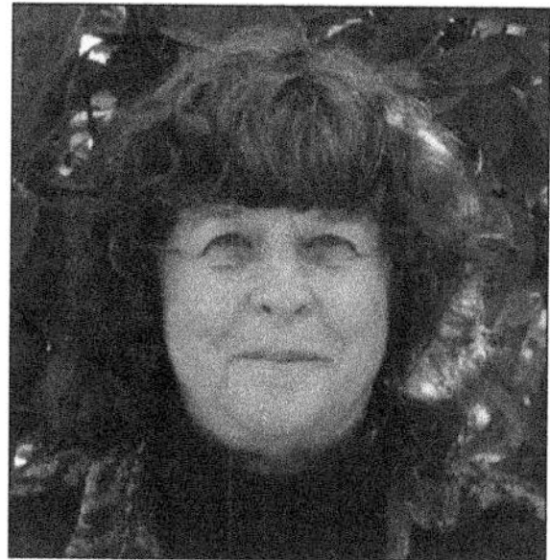

SUSAN FOX, *Coastal floodplain*

foxstudio.biz | sketchwild.com

Facebook, Instagram, Twitter, Pinterest, Etsy and RedBubble

Susan Fox has worked in art-related fields for over forty years. For the last 20, she's mostly painted in oil, specializing in animals and the natural world. A world traveler, she keeps sketchbooks of her travels, including trips to Mongolia, Kenya, Europe, and locations in the US. She has a BFA in Illustration from the Academy of Art University in San Francisco. She lives on an acre in Redwood country in northern CA with her husband, two rough collie dogs, and two cats.

LUCY GAGLIARDO, *Beauty in the estuary*

Lucy Gagliardo lives in the Finger Lakes area of NY. She grew up on Long Island, loving all that lives in the bays and ocean. She studied biology at Southampton College (now Stony Brook University) where she was introduced to scientific illustration. Over the years she has taken many art classes and workshops, focusing on natural science illustration. She worked as a freelance illustrator and a research technician in an immunology and parasitology laboratory. She's been a member of the Guild of Natural Science Illustrators since 1980. Now retired, she is dabbling in different media, trying to capture the amazing natural world and sharing with the community through exhibits and teaching.

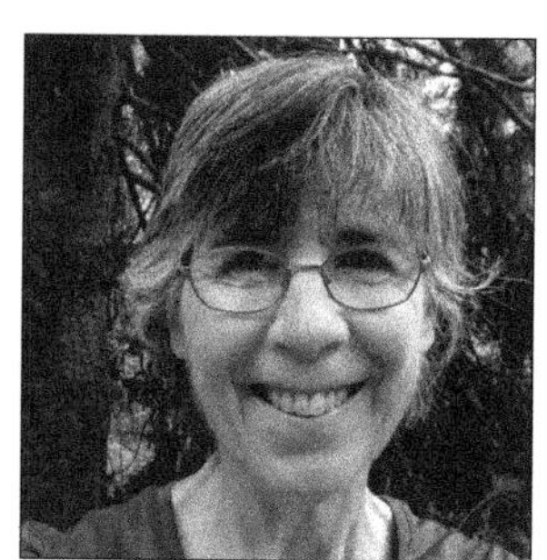

MADISON HENLINE, *Sunning on the sea*
madisonhenline.com, @rhunevild on Instagram and Twitter

Though currently based in Dallas, TX, Madison grew up in Savannah, Georgia and attended SCAD. She graduated with a degree in Sequential Art, though these days she focuses more on paleoart and sculpture than comic books.

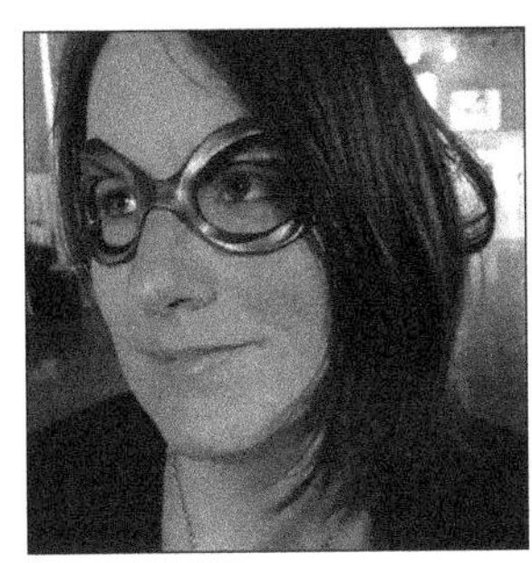

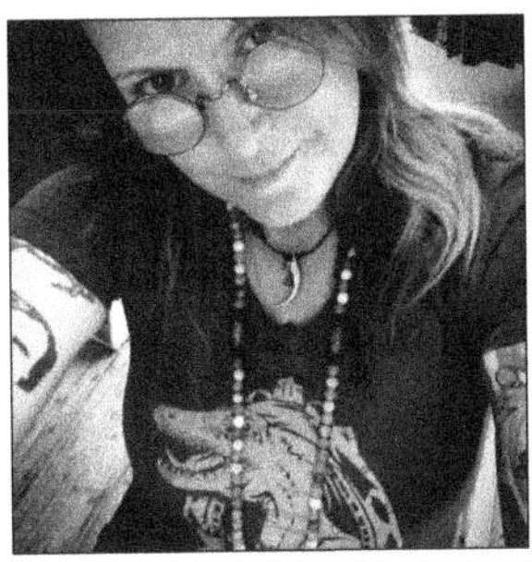

CHARON HENNING, *Growing up on the beach*
charonhenning.com, keiphavian.com

Charon Henning is a location-independent scientific illustrator and fine artist. A member of the Guild of Natural Science Illustrators, she enjoys working in the areas of vertebrate paleontology, osteology and ornithology in a variety of media. She holds an Associate's Degree in Fine Art from Prince George's Community College and a Bachelor's Degree in Individualized Studies: Multimedia Storytelling from George Mason University, where she earned the faculty award for Most Creative Capstone Project.

SAMI HERNANDEZ, *From the river to the sea, From the sea to the river, Diamond in the marsh, Winter vacation*
samihernandez.com

Samantha Hernandez is a sequential artist living in Prosper, TX. She has fun creating her illustrated children's book series, drawing comics, and teaching art to kids after school! She studied at SCAD in beautiful Savannah, GA.

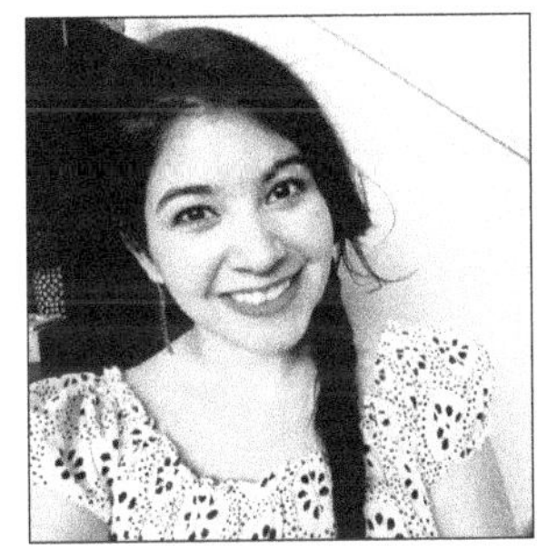

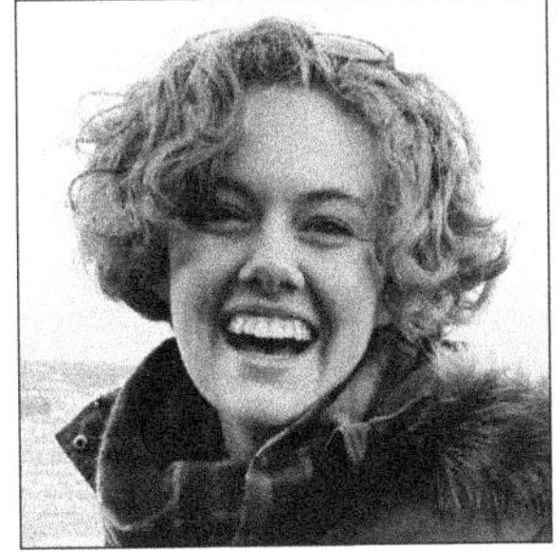

CLARA HUNT, *Blending with the sand, Estuary nursery*
@clara_fied27 on Instagram

Clara Hunt is an illustrator from West Bend, WI. She is currently a senior at SCAD, with an emphasis is in Publication Design. Moving forward in her career, Clara would love to be involved in projects related to editorial work, book illustration, and impactful opportunities like this coloring book!

TRENTON JUNG, *Along the shore*
trentonwjung.com | @trenton.jung

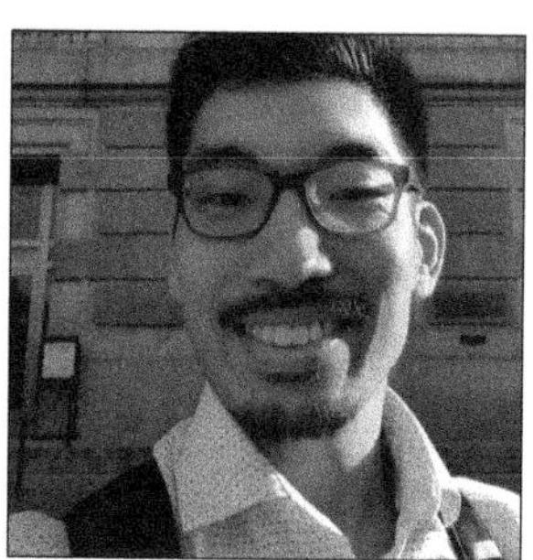

Trenton Jung is a natural science illustrator based in Alexandria, VA. Born and raised outside of Los Angeles, CA, the sun and ocean play an influential role in his work. He received his BFA in Illustration from the Maryland Institute College of Art and is an active member of the Guild of Natural Science Illustrators. Trenton's work reflects his deep interest in nature and organic forms, focusing on the unseen and unnoticed aspects of nature. He uses a variety of mediums, including watercolor, graphite, colored pencil, ink, and gouache. His work has been featured in *Smithsonian Magazine*, at the University of Riverside, CA, and exhibted in Washington D.C., Baltimore, Fullerton, CA and Brisbane, Australia.

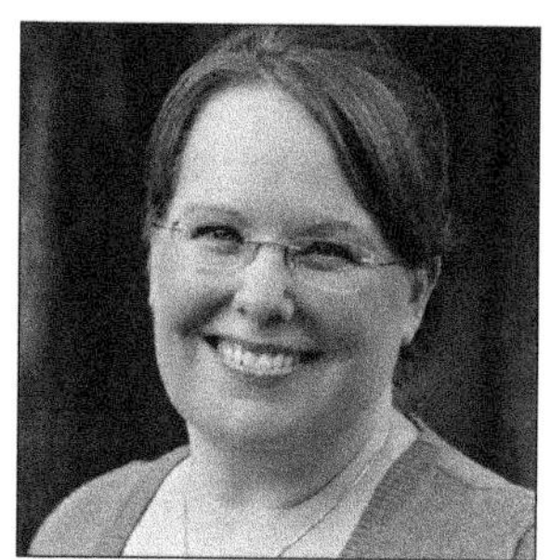

JENNIFER LANDIN, *Hidden in the rubble*
rednewtgallery.com, jmlandin.com

Art is a great medium for sharing information. Jennifer uses drawing when teaching biology courses at NC State University. Drawing increases interest in science topics, focuses observation on detail, and helps in processing complex ideas. In her creative work, she often spotlights small, squishy, or scaly organisms. Larger, more charismatic creatures receive so much attention, yet insects and other invertebrates are far more numerous and ecologically important. Her studio is based in Cary, NC and her work is exhibited internationally.

CATHY MEYER, *Author*

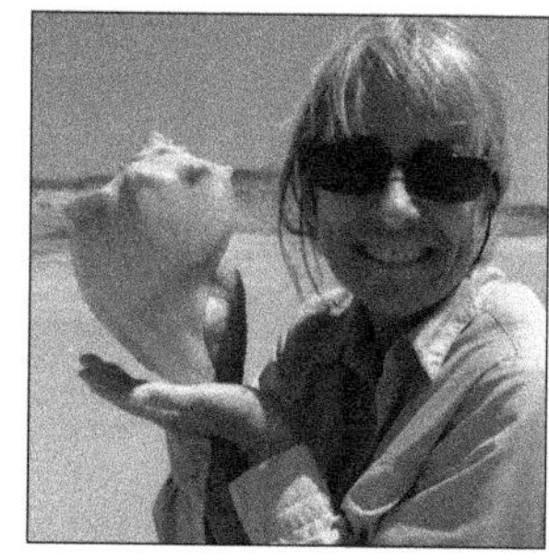

Cathy Meyer is a coastal naturalist and writer. She has a Bachelor of Arts in English from Fairmont State University. With an insatiable curiosity about the coastal environment, she has always been drawn to the natural wonders of the seashore. Countless hours have been spent over 40 years, walking coastal beaches in North Carolina and many other shorelines in the United States and beyond. Cathy lives close to Masonboro Island, NC.

TIFFANY MILLER RUSSELL, *Marathon swimmers, Tidal creek*

wildlifeinpaper.com

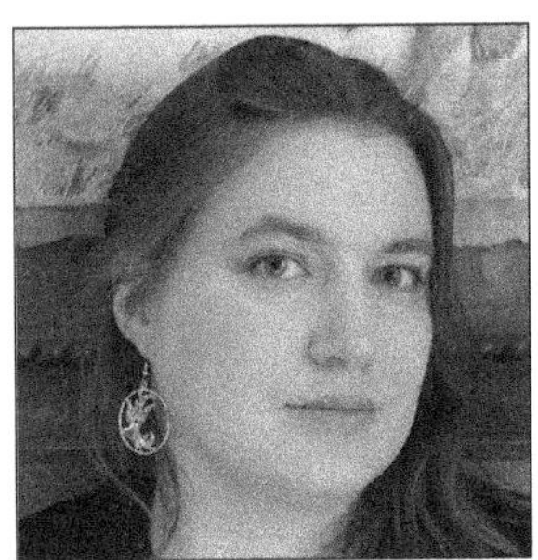

Tiffany Miller Russell has a love for the unique and unusual that has lead her to into both her study of the natural world, and her depiction of it in cut paper sculpture. Her paper sculptures have won her numerous awards from the likes of *Artists' Magazine* and the Society of Animal Artists, including a travel grant to Trinidad and Tobago. She shows regularly in juried museum exhibitions and fine art galleries, and two of her works are included in the permanent Contemporary Art collection of the Cheyenne Frontier Days Old West Museum. She resides in Denver, CO.

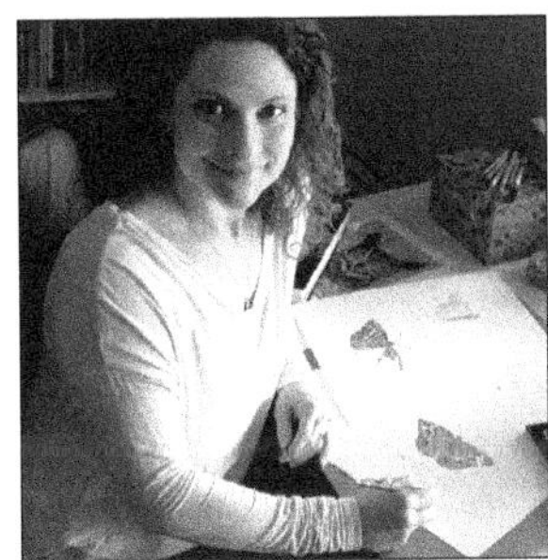

CHRISTINA SPENCE MORGAN, *Armed with venom*

christinamorganillustration.com

Christina Spence Morgan is an early-career illustrator originally from FL, currently based in the DC area. Once a theatre major, she turned her back on the stage forever after seeing a kelp forest for the first time in an aquarium, deciding to pursue a biology degree then and there. She earned a Bachelors of Science in Marine Biology from the University of California Santa Cruz in 2007, and a Professional Certificate in Museum Studies from CU Boulder in 2010. She has worked in both natural history museum collections and aquariums, and is now a student of the Science Illustration Distance Learning Program. She still loves kelp forests, and enjoys drawing marine invertebrates most of all, particularly for her two little jelly-loving kids.

ANNE THERESE J. NAMOCATCAT, *Summer love, Sandollar (title page)*

annenamocatcat.com | @namocatcat.illustration on instagram

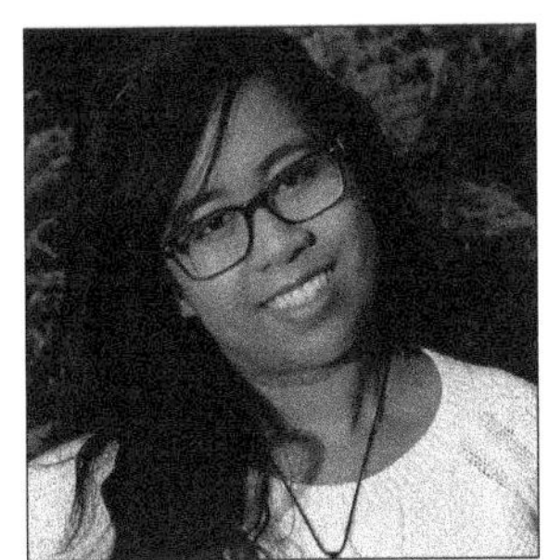

Anne Therese J. Namocatcat is a trained scientific illustrator from Long Island, NY. She received her Master of Fine Art in Medical Illustration from Rochester Institute of Technology (RIT). She also holds a Bachelor of Science in biology from La Salle University. When she isn't illustrating nature or various medical anomalies, you might find her wandering her local beaches in search of migrating shorebirds.

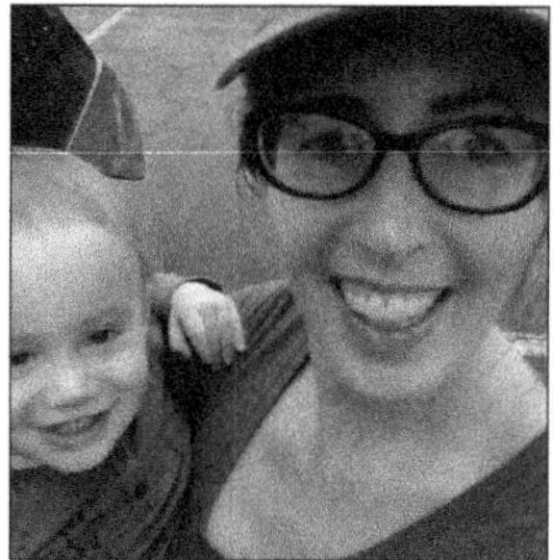

CORDELIA NORRIS, *Author, Oysters and ibis in the Marsh (half title page), Beach beginnings*
lunacreates.com, behance.net/lunac

Cordelia is lead creative and founder of Luna Creative, an award-winning design studio providing working with values-driven organizations. She has a Master's in Illustration from SCAD and undergraduate degrees in Graphic Design, Studio Art, and Art History. Her work's been recognized with awards from American Institute of Graphic Artists (AIGA), American Advertising Federation (AAF), *Applied Arts*, and exhibited around the country. She lives in Wilmington, NC, with her adorable family (husband, baby boy, dog, and cat). Also the author of *Hatchlings* in 2018, *All Along the Atlantic* is her second book in the Coloring Nature series.

KARA PERILLI, *Sea gardener, Music in the marsh*
karaperilli.myportfolio.com

Kara is a freelance scientific illustrator and designer who works in both digital and traditional media. She graduated with a degree in Scientific Illustration from Arcadia University, and is currently based in the greater Philadelphia area. The artwork she produces covers a diverse array of subjects, though projects focusing on botanical subjects and outer space always inspire her. She aims to promote science education and provide resources with impactful visuals and information for a range of audiences.

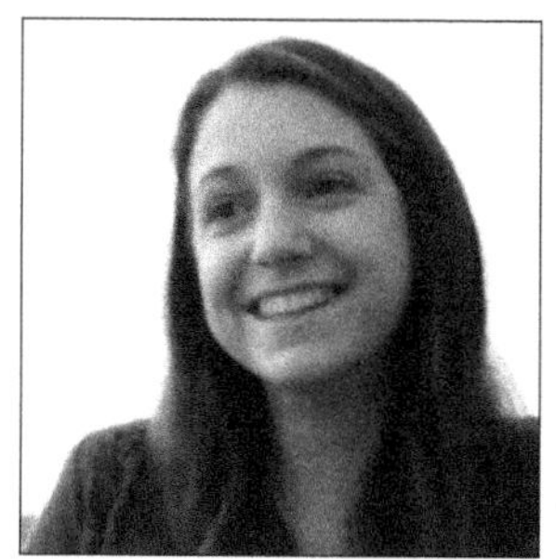

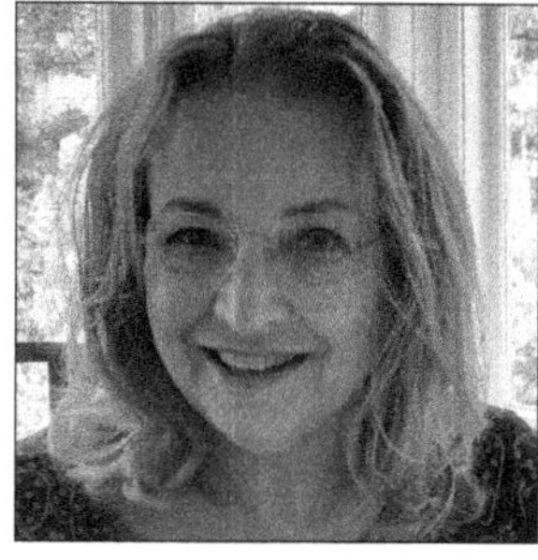

SUELLEN PEROLD, *Datura (introduction facing page)*

Suellen's interest in botanical art began after a career in art education, childbirth/child photography, and political campaign organizing. She received a Certificate in Botanical Art from Wellesley College, a BA in Education from UMass Amherst and a MEd from Stanford. She loves to start her day drawing and deeply experiencing the natural world, and feels lucky to be doing so on the Eastern Seaboard.

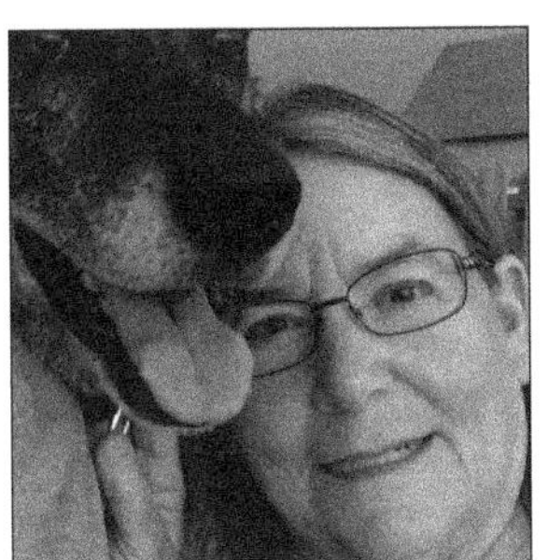

ANNE RUNYON, *Tidal salt marsh, Deep in the cypress swamp*
annerunyon.com | scbwi.org/members-public/anne-runyon
Anne Runyon lives in Garner, NC. She earned her BA in studio art from Carleton College, and her MA from the University of Minnesota, studying design and children's literature in their Kerlan Collection. She works on paper with ink, watercolor, and colored pencil, creating illustrations for environmental educational publications, and exhibits in North Carolina. She writes and illustrates children's books, creates woodcut prints, and paper sculpture craft activities. She belongs to the Guild of Natural Science Illustrators, Carolinas chapter, the Society of Children's Book Writers and Illustrators, and several conservation groups in North Carolina.

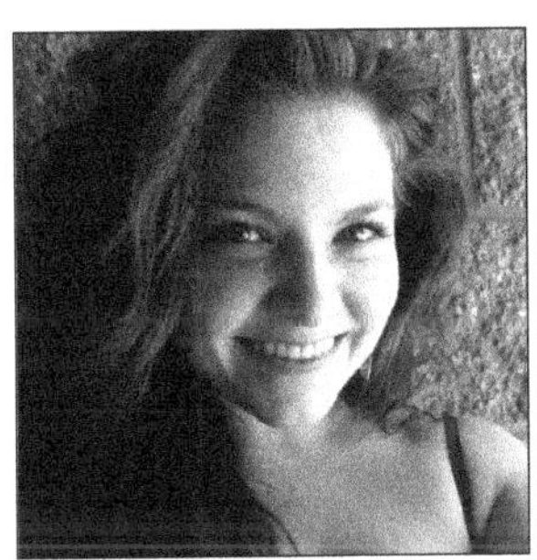

TINA SCHOFIELD, *Open ocean, Underwater forests*
tinaschofield.com
Tina Schofield is an independent illustrator and textile designer based out of Bucks County, PA. She received a Bachelors degree in Fine Arts with a focus on Illustration from SCAD in 2011. Her work can be found in designer boutiques, retail stores, as well as the Vatican and the White House. She loves to cook, dance, ride horses, explore the outdoors, and travel any chance she gets. She also is a wildlife and environmental conservationist and volunteers for animal rescues.

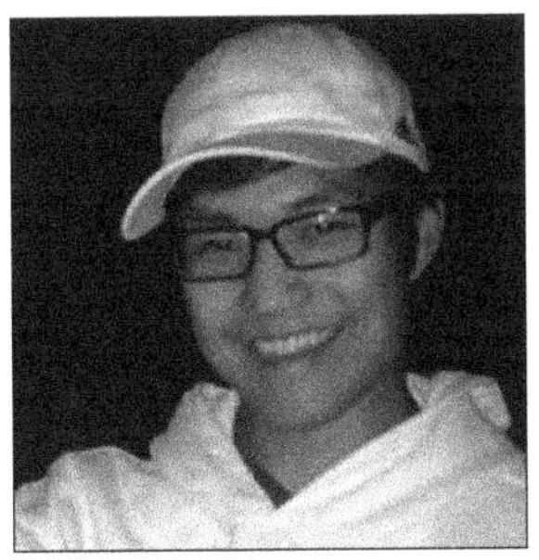

ZACH SCHRAGE, *Hidden among the reeds, Invasive species*
artstation.com/zachschrage
Zachary Schrage is an Illustrator based in Long Island, NY. He is currently studying drawing and painting at the Atelier at Flowerfield as an apprentice.

ALISA SINGH, *Stars of the sea*
linktr.ee/jellyfish_and_stone

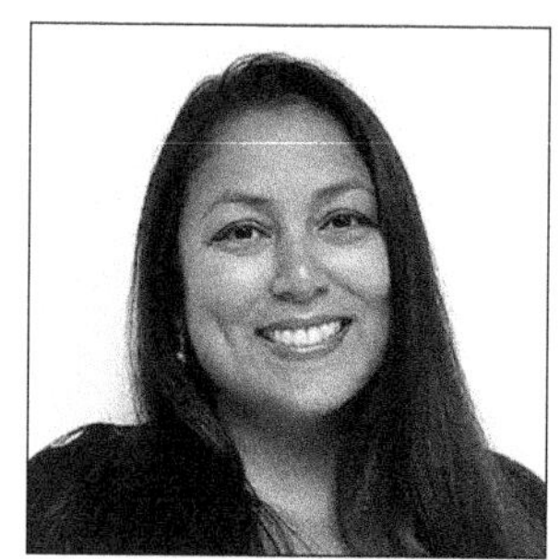

Alisa Singh of Jellyfish & Stone Studio is a natural science illustrator and educator based in Toronto, Canada. She takes great delight in sharing the natural world with others through her illustrations. Alisa is fascinated by marvels, both small and large, in the world around us. She's particularly interested in life in the deep sea, where there is still so much to learn. She studied illustration at the Ontario College of Art and Design and, after a short time freelancing, switched gears to pursue a successful career in the corporate world. After more than a decade, she returned to illustration. Alisa primarily works in pen and ink, watercolour, and acrylics.

AMANDA SURVESKI, *Charismatic cetacean*
amandasurveski.com

Amanda Surveski is a freelance illustrator and designer from CT, creating work influenced by the natural world. Prompted by a love of animals from an early age and a diverse backyard growing up, she constantly learns, explores, and admires her surroundings. Her work focuses on highlighting the beauty and diversity of the natural world, from our own backyards to the furthest reaches of the globe. She graduated from SCAD with a BFA in Illustration and a minor in Scientific Illustration.

AMY YEAGER, *Nesting island*
tusgart.weebly.com | @tusg.art on instagram
tusg.art on facebook

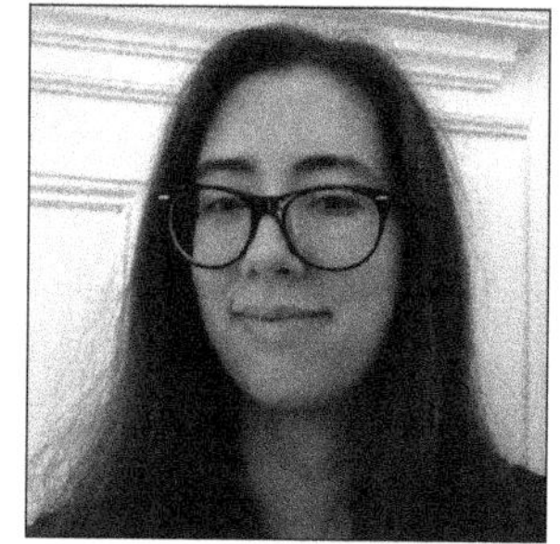

Amy Yeager is a Boston-based artist, illustrator, and land snail enthusiast. She attended Clark University where she designed her own major in Scientific Illustration. The majority of Amy's professional experience lies in mycological illustration, though her favorite subjects are insects and strange fish. In addition, she paints abstracted food and viscera drawing inspiration from wet, squishy surfaces and gross pathology specimens.

websites

Animal Diversity Web. www.animaldiversity.org (accessed September-November 2019).

Audubon. www.audubon.org (accessed September-November 2019).

Chesapeake Bay Program. www.chesapeakebay.net (accessed September-November 2019).

The Cornell Lab of Ornithology, All About Birds. www.allaboutbirds.org (accessed September-November 2019).

Sea Turtle Conservancy. www.conserveturtles.org (accessed September-November 2019).

NOAA Fisheries. www.fisheries.noaa.gov (accessed September-November 2019).

Jelly Watch. www.jellywatch.org (accessed September-November 2019).

National Geographic. www.nationalgeographic.com (accessed September-November 2019).

The National Wildlife Federation. www.nwf.org (accessed September-November 2019).

North Carolina Coastal Federation. www.nccoast.org (accessed September-November 2019).

books and articles:

Casey, Susan. *Voices in the Ocean.* New York, New York: Doubleday, 2015.

Ehrlich, Paul R., David S. Dobkin, and Darryl Wheye. *The Birder's Handbook: A Field Guide to the Natural History of North American Birds.* New York, New York: Simon and Schuster, Fireside, 1988.

Hosier, Paul E. *Seacoast Plants of the Carolinas.* Chapel Hill, NC: University of North Carolina Press, 2018.

Karlansky, Mark. *Cod: A Biography of the Fish that Changed the World.* London: Penguin Books, 1998.

Meyer, Peter. *Blue Crabs: Catch 'em, Cook 'em, Eat 'em.* Wilmington, NC: Avian-Cetacean Press. 2003, revised 2012.

Meyer, Peter. *Nature Guide to the Carolina Coast; Common Birds, Crabs, Shells, Fish, and the Entities of the Coastal Environment.* Wilmington, NC: Avian-Cetacean Press. 2010, 2016, 2nd edition.

Meyer, Peter. *The Mud Toad Makes its Mark.* Wildlife in North Carolina, Volume 69(1), March 2005, pp. 14-19. (Digital issue available State Library of North Carolina: digital.ncdcr.gov/cdm/fullbrowser/collection/p16062coll4/id/23740/rv/compoundobject/cpd/23784)

Meyer, Peter and Cathy. *Just When you Thought it was Safe...* Wildlife in North Carolina, Volume 58(8), August 1994, pp. 25-27. (Revised and reprinted, *Hazardous Marine Animals of the Carolina Coast.* Wilmington, NC: Avian-Cetacean Press, 2015. aviancetaceanpress.com/hazardous-marine-animals-of-the-carolina-coast/

Peterson, Roger Tory. *Peterson Field Guide to Birds of Eastern and Central North America.* New York, New York: Huffton Mifflin Harcourt Publishing Company, 2010. Sixth edition.

Pyenson, Nick. *Spying on whales: The past, present, and future of earth's most awesome creatures.* London: Penguin Books, 2018.

www.ingramcontent.com/pod-product-compliance
Ingram Content Group UK Ltd.
Pitfield, Milton Keynes, MK11 3LW, UK
UKHW062009290726
14090UKWH00022B/1472